MW00678221

Anatomy Notebooking Journal

for

Exploring Creation with Human Anatomy and Physiology

by
Jeannie Fulbright

Anatomy Notebooking Journal

Published by
Apologia Educational Ministries, Inc.
1106 Meridian Plaza, Suite 220/340
Anderson, IN 46016

www.apologia.com

Manufactured in the United States of America
Fourth Printing: April 2013

ISBN: 978-1-935495-15-4

Printed by Courier Printing, Kendallville, IN

Cover Design by Kim Williams

All Biblical quotations are from the New American Standard Bible, King James Version, New International Version or New King James Version
Cover photos licensed through Shutterstock
Sebastian Kaulitzki, Elena Kalistratova, Alexander Vasilyev, Artman, HKahn

Photo Credits

Images by Shutterstock: 11, 13 (Sebastian Kaulitzki, Elena Kalistratova, Alexander Vasilyev, Artman, HKahn), 28, 29, 38, 39, 49, 73, 74, 75, 94, 95, 104, 149, 161 (Matthew Cole), 105, 49 (Tara Urbach), 139 (Andrea Danti), A46
Images by Jupiter Images: 16, 17, 20, 21, 24, 26, 34, 36, 37, 44, 46, 47, 56, 58, 59, 60, 63, 69, 71, 72, 77, 80, 82, 83, 90, 92, 99, 103, 107 (bottom), 109, 113, 116 (bottom), 121, 123, 125 (top), 132, 134, 135, 143, 147, 148, 150, 151, 153, 159, 160, 167, 171, A1, A11, A12, A19, A21, A49, A50
Images in the Public Domain: 49 (middle, left) 74 (middle), 107 (top), 119, 116, 126, A37, A38, A42 (NEI), A44 (Patrick J. Lynch, medical illustrator; C. Carl Jaffe, MD, cardiologist), A51, A53
Images by Crestock: 84, 93, 94, 95 (bottom), 98, A5, A7, A29, A31, A45
Images by Megan Fruchte: 96, 178 (top)
Images © 2007 Wolters Kluwer Health | Lippincott Williams and Wilkins: 31, 49 (bottom), 74 (bottom), 105, 114, 116 and 117 (top), 124, 125(bottom), 174, 178 (bottom), A5 (bottom), A17, A39, A40
Images by Kim Williams: Cover, 13
Images by Jeannie Fulbright: Cover, 13

Fonts used with permission/license from:

www.4yeo.com FYO Out
My Fonts.com: Cutout std, Geometr885, Harvestmoon, Intellectaborders, Mariaballeinitials, Otherworld, Superstarlike, Trajan, Treasury Gold, Ulma, Waltari, Zapfino, Aeronaut
Apostrophic Labs: Endor, Futurex Apocalypse, Halcion, McKloud, Merkin, Powderfinger,
Laurie Szujewska: Giddyup,
Educational Fontware: HWT cursive, HWT print
Font Diner.com: Starburst Lanes
Brian Eaters Font Co: Musicals

Note from the Author

Welcome to the wonderful adventure in learning called "Notebooking." This notebooking journal correlates with Apologia's *Exploring Creation with Human Anatomy and Physiology,* by Jeannie Fulbright and Brooke Ryan, M.D. The activities in this journal provide everything your child needs to complete the assignments in *Exploring Creation with Human Anatomy and Physiology* and more. It will serve as your child's individual notebook. You only need to provide scissors, glue, colored pencils, a stapler and a few brass fasteners.

The concept of notebooking is not a new one. In fact, keeping notebooks was the primary way the learned men of our past educated themselves, from Leonardo Da Vinci and Christopher Columbus to George Washington, John Quincy Adams and Meriwether Lewis. These men and many others of their time were avid notebookers. As we know, they were also much more advanced in their knowledge—even as teens—than we are today. George Washington was a licensed surveyor during his teenage years, and John Quincy Adams graduated from law school at age 17.

It would be wise for us to emulate the methods of education of these great men, rather than the failing methods used in our schools today. Common modern methods, namely fill-in-the-blank and matching worksheets, do not fully engage the student's mind. Studies show that we remember only 5% of what we hear, 50% of what we see and hear and 90% of what we see, hear and do. When we participate in activities that correspond with learning, we increase our retention exponentially. This is exactly what the Anatomy Notebooking Journal is designed to do—offer engaging learning activities to increase your student's retention.

The National Center for Educational Statistics shows us that American school children, by twelfth grade, rank at the bottom of international assessments, and do not even know 50% of what students in top-ranked countries know. As home educators, we have the opportunity to discard methods that are detrimental and ineffective and adopt the methods which will genuinely educate our children.

In addition to academic achievement, notebooking offers many benefits to students and parents. For students, it provides an opportunity to uniquely express themselves as they learn. It also provides a treasured memento of educational endeavors. For parents, it is a record of the year's studies and can easily be transferred to a portfolio if needed.

This journal will make notebooking easier for both you and your student by supplying a plethora of templates, hands-on crafts and projects, additional experiment ideas, and many activities that will engage your student in learning. It will prove invaluable in helping students create a wonderful keepsake of all they learned in human anatomy and physiology. Remember that *everything in this notebooking journal is optional.* Because it will serve as your student's own unique notebook, you may customize it by simply tearing out the activity pages that you choose not to use. You, as the teacher, will decide what truly benefits your student's learning experience, encourages a love for learning and builds his confidence in science. Every child is different, learns differently and will respond differently to the array of activities provided here. Use discernment in how many of the activities and assignments you use with your child. Your goal is not to complete every activity but to make learning a joy.

However, as a seasoned home educator, let me encourage you not to attempt to do every single activity in this notebooking journal. Choose the projects and activities that will be enjoyable and inspire a love of learning. If something is a drudgery, it will not serve to increase your student's retention, but will only discourage his enjoyment of science–resulting in an unmotivated learner.

It is my hope and prayer that you and your students will benefit from your studies this year, growing closer to God as you learn of His creation, and finding joy in the learning process.

Warmly,

Table of Contents

Descriptions and Instructions for Each Page in Journal 6
Daily Schedule/ Reading Guide 8
Journal Owner Cover Page 13
Personal Person Project 15

Lesson 1 Introduction to Anatomy and Physiology 16
Fascinating Facts about Anatomy and Physiology 16
Cell Anatomy 18
What Do You Remember? 19
Notebooking Activity: History of Anatomy 20
Vocabulary Crossword 22
Scripture Copywork 24
Minibook Paste Page 26
More to Explore 27
Project Page 28

Lesson 2 The Skeletal System 29
Fascinating Facts about the Skeletal System 29
What Do You Remember? 30
Notebooking Activity: Label a Skeleton 31
Vocabulary Crossword 32
Scripture Copywork 34
Minibook Paste Page 36
More to Explore 37
Project Page 38
Scientific Speculation Sheet 39

Lesson 3 The Muscular System 40
Fascinating Facts About the Muscular System 40
What Do You Remember? 42
Notebooking Activity: Muscle Times 43
Vocabulary Crossword 44
Scripture Copywork 46
Minibook Paste Page 48
More to Explore 49
Project Page 50
Scientific Speculation Sheet 51

Lesson 4 The Digestive and Renal Systems 52
Fascinating Facts About the Digestive System 52
What Do You Remember? 54
Notebooking Activity: Comic Strip 55
Vocabulary Crossword 56
Scripture Copywork 60
Minibook Paste Page 62
More to Explore 63
Project Page 64

Lesson 5 Health and Nutrition 65
Fascinating Facts About Nutrition 65
What Do You Remember? 66
Try This! Page 67
Notebooking Project: Food Pyramid 68
Notebooking Activity: Dinner Menu 69
Vocabulary Crossword 72
Scripture Copywork 76
Minibook Paste Page 78
More to Explore 79
Project Page 80
Scientific Speculation Sheet 81

Lesson 6 The Respiratory System 82
Fascinating Facts About the Respiratory System 82
What Do You Remember? 84
Notebooking Activity: Smoking Speech 85
Vocabulary Crossword 86
Scripture Copywork 88
Minibook Paste Page 90
More to Explore 91
Project Page 92

Lesson 7 Life in the Blood 93
Fascinating Facts About Blood 93
What Do You Remember? 95
Notebooking Activity: Blood Components 96
Notebooking Activity: Apologia of Faith 97
Vocabulary Crossword 98
Scripture Copywork 100
Minibook Paste Page 102
More to Explore 103
Project Page 104

Lesson 8 The Cardiovascular System 105
Fascinating Facts About the Cardiovascular System 105
How Blood Flows Through the Heart 107
What Do You Remember? 108
Notebooking Activity: Advertisement 109
Scripture Copywork 110
Vocabulary Crossword 112
Minibook Paste Page 114
More to Explore 115
Project Page 116

Lesson 9 The Nervous and Endocrine Systems 117
Fascinating Facts About the Nervous System 117
What Do Your Remember? 119
Notebooking Activity: Label a Brain and Neuron 120
Notebooking Activity: Venn Diagram 121
Scripture Copywork 122
Vocabulary Crossword 124
More to Explore 127
Project Page 128
Paste Page 129

Lesson 10 The Nervous System Extended 130
Fascinating Facts About the Nervous System 130
What Do You Remember? 131
Notebooking Activity: Brain and Spinal Cord 132
Notebooking Activity: Cerebral Lobes 134
Vocabulary Crossword 135
Scripture Copywork 136
Minibook Paste Page 138
More to Explore 139
Project Page 140

Table of Contents

Lesson 11 Your Senses 141
    Fascinating Facts About Your Senses 141
    What Do You Remember? 142
    Notebooking Activity: Diagram of Eye 143
    Vocabulary Crossword 144
    Scripture Copywork 148
    Minibook Paste Page 150
    More to Explore 151
    Project Page 152

Lesson 12 The Integumentary System 153
    Fascinating Facts About the Integumentary System 153
    What Do You Remember? 155
    Notebooking Activity: Diagram of Skin 156
    Notebooking Activity: Fingerprints 157
    Try This! Page 158
    Braille Alphabet Activity 159
    Try This! Page 161
    Scripture Copywork 162
    Vocabulary Crossword 164
    Minibook Paste Page 166
    More to Explore 167
    Project Page 168
    Scientific Speculation Sheet 169

Lesson 13 The Lymphatic and Immune Systems 170
    Fascinating Facts About the Immune System 170
    What Do You Remember? 171
    Notebooking Activity: Pathogens and Defense Pages 172
    Scripture Copywork 174
    Vocabulary Crossword 176
    Minibook Paste Page 180
    More to Explore 181
    Project Page 182
    Scientific Speculation Sheet 183

Lesson 14 Growth and Development 184
    Fascinating Facts About Growth and Development 184
    What Do You Remember? 185
    Notebooking Activity: Stages of Development 186
    Possible Purpose Page 187
    Scripture Copywork 188
    Vocabulary Crossword 190
    Minibook Paste Page 192
    More to Explore 193
    Project Page 194

Final Review Questions 195
Vocabulary Crossword Solutions 197
Final Review Solutions 200
Field Trip Sheets 201
Minibooks ....Appendix
Personal Person Templates ....Appendix

Anatomy Notebooking Journal

Below are descriptions of a suggested schedule and the activities included in this notebooking journal. The first three activities are taken directly from the coursework contained in *Exploring Creation with Human Anatomy and Physiology*. The others are additional optional activities coordinating with the book.

Suggested Schedule

A suggested schedule for reading the *Exploring Creation with Human Anatomy and Physiology* text and completing the activities contained in the book and in this journal has been provided. Though not every student or parent will choose to utilize the schedule, those who do may find it very beneficial. Some parents will appreciate having their student's daily reading and assignments organized for them. Older students will find it easy to complete the book and journal by following the schedule on their own. Though the suggested schedule provides for the human anatomy and physiology course to be completed in twenty-eight weeks, two days per week, it is flexible and can be made to fit your goals. The course can be expedited by completing three or four days of science per week. You can lengthen the course by studying science only one day per week. If you wish to do the extra activities found in the More to Explore pages, still another day of science can be added. Above all, use the suggested schedule in a way that best suits your family.

Fascinating Facts

Exploring Creation with Human Anatomy and Physiology contains many facts, ideas and interesting notions. Although oral (verbal) narration is an effective means for retention, your student may wish to record some of the information either through drawing or writing. The Fascinating Facts pages can be used for written narrations. Some of the lessons provide two Fascinating Facts pages for your student's use. If your student is an avid writer, you can access more Fascinating Facts pages to print (free of charge) on the Apologia website. To do so, simply login to www.apologia.com/bookextras and type in this password: Godmadeyou. These additional pages can be included in this notebooking journal by simply stapling them onto one of the existing Fascinating Facts pages.

What Do You Remember? Review Questions

These review questions are the same questions asked in the "What Do You Remember?" section found in each lesson of the book. They can be answered orally (verbally) or, for older students, as a written narration assignment. For co-ops or classroom use, these questions may also serve as a way to evaluate how much the students have retained from the reading. However, I would encourage you to review the material with the students before giving the questions as a written narration assignment. This will encourage better retention of the material and increase both the students' confidence and their ability to restate their learning. The answers to the review questions can be found on pages 253 through 257 of *Exploring Creation with Human Anatomy and Physiology*.

Notebooking Assignments, Activities and Projects

The lessons in *Exploring Creation with Human Anatomy and Physiology* offer suggested notebooking assignments, activities and projects typically found at the end of each lesson. Provided in this journal are templates (blank pages with lines for writing or space for drawing) which your student can use for completing these activities. Colored pencils can be used to encourage creative, high quality work. Some projects require the student to use a Scientific Speculation Sheet. These sheets have been included in this notebooking journal. Drawings or pictures of the projects can be pasted onto the Scientific Speculation Sheets.

Scripture Copywork

Incorporating the Word of God in your science studies through Scripture Copywork will provide many benefits to your student. It will encourage stronger faith and memorization of Scripture, as well as better writing, spelling and grammar skills. Each lesson has a corresponding verse for your child to copy, which may be printed or written in cursive.

Vocabulary Crosswords

If you desire to expand your child's studies with vocabulary activities, the Vocabulary Crosswords can be used to review the new words and concepts mentioned in the lesson. Remember, working with the vocabulary in this manner is not a "test" of your child's knowledge, but should be viewed as a reinforcement and reminder of what he has learned. The answers to the Vocabulary Crosswords can be found on pages 197 through 199.

Project Pages

Many of the projects and experiments in *Exploring Creation with Human Anatomy and Physiology* are "hands-on" and therefore cannot be preserved in a notebook. Each lesson in this notebooking journal provides a Project Page in which your student can write about what he did and learned from the various projects and experiments contained in the course-work. Be sure to take pictures of the finished products and glue them onto the Project Pages. Your child will enjoy looking back and remembering the fun he had learning human anatomy and physiology!

Cut and Fold Miniature Books

At the back of this journal, you will find Cut and Fold Miniature Book craft activities that correspond with the reading. These miniature books are designed to review the concepts learned in each lesson. Writing lines are provided on the miniature books so your students can record the information they have learned. Some books ask for specific information. Others do not and allow the students to record the facts they found most interesting. Students will cut out the pattern, write what they have learned in the designated places, then assemble the books according to the directions. Paste Pages are included in this journal for each miniature book activity. The Paste Pages provide a place for your students to preserve and display their Cut and Fold Miniature Books. Instructions are included for pasting the miniature books onto the Paste Pages.

These books are entirely optional. Some students thrive with the hands-on approach, while other students do not benefit academically from this type of activity. Allow your students to try the Cut and Fold Miniature Books to see if they enjoy learning in this way.

More to Explore

The More to Explore suggestions are designed to give your student additional ideas and activities that might enhance his studies such as: experiments, hands-on activities, research and living book titles, as well as audio and video resources. Because these assignments are entirely optional, they are not included in the suggested schedule for completing the notebooking journal.

Field Trip Sheets

Your family may wish to further enhance your studies by visiting a science museum or perhaps the Bodies Exhibit. Field Trip Sheets are provided at the back of this notebooking journal to record your visits. You can make a pocket on the back of these sheets to hold any brochures or additional information you receive. Simply glue three edges (sides and bottom) of a half piece of construction paper to the bottom of the Field Trip Sheet.

Final Review

At the end of this journal are 50 questions that review the entire course. They can be answered orally or in writing. This is an optional activity; however, I believe your students would be pleasantly surprised to see how much they know about human anatomy and physiology after answering the questions. The answers to the Final Review can be found on page 200.

Week	Day 1	Day 2
1	**Lesson 1 - Introduction to Human Anatomy & Physiology** Read *T pp. 19-22* & Narrate Begin working on Fascinating Facts about the History of Anatomy *NJ pp. 16-17* Try This! *T p. 21* Read *T pp. 22-24* & Narrate Try This! *T p. 23*	Read *T pp. 24-26* & Narrate Try This! *T p. 26* Read *T pp. 26-28* & Narrate Drawing: Cell Anatomy *T p. 26, NJ p. 18*
2	**Lesson 1 - Introduction to Human Anatomy & Physiology** Read *T pp. 29-31* & Narrate Read *T pp. 31-33* & Narrate Written Narration: What Do You Remember? *T p. 33, NJ p. 19* Notebooking Activity: History of Anatomy *T p. 33, NJ pp. 20-21*	Personal Person Project: Create Personal Person *T p. 33, NJ p. 15* Vocabulary Crossword *NJ pp. 22-23* Scripture Copywork *NJ pp. 24-25* Cell Minibook *NJ Appendix p. A 7* Project: Edible Cell *T p. 35, NJ p. 28*
3	**Lesson 2 - The Skeletal System** Read *T pp. 37-40* & Narrate Begin working on Fascinating Facts about the Skeletal System *NJ p. 29* Try This! *T p. 37* Try This! *T p. 38* Read *T pp. 41-42* & Narrate	Read *T pp. 42-44* & Narrate Try This! *T p. 43* Read *T pp. 45-48* & Narrate Read *T pp. 49-50* & Narrate Try This! *T p. 49* Try This! *T p. 50*
4	**Lesson 2 - The Skeletal System** Read *T pp. 51-52* & Narrate Try This! *T p. 51* Written Narration: What Do You Remember? *T p. 52, NJ p. 30* Notebooking Activity: Label a Skeleton *T p. 52, NJ p. 31*	Personal Person Project: Add some bones *T p. 52 NJ p. 15* Vocabulary Crossword *NJ pp. 32-33* Scripture Copywork *NJ pp. 34-35* Bones Minibook *NJ Appendix p. A 11* Experiment: Analyzing a Chicken Bone *T p. 53, NJ p. 39*
5	**Lesson 3 - The Muscular System** Read *T pp. 55-57* & Narrate Try This! *T p. 56* Begin working on Fascinating Facts about the Muscular System *NJ pp. 40-41* Read *T pp. 57-60* & Narrate Try This! *T p. 58*	Try This! *T p. 61* Read *T pp. 61-64* & Narrate Try This! *T p. 62* Try This! *T p. 63*
6	**Lesson 3 - The Muscular System** Read *T pp. 64-66* & Narrate Try This! *T p. 66* Written Narration: What Do You Remember? *T p. 66, NJ p. 42* Personal Person Project: Add some muscles *T p. 67, NJ p. 15*	Notebooking Activity: The Muscle Times *T p. 67, NJ p. 43* Vocabulary Crossword *NJ pp. 44-45* Scripture Copywork *NJ pp. 46-47* Muscles Minibook *NJ Appendix p. A 13* Experiment: Growing Muscle *T p. 67, NJ p. 51*
7	**Lesson 4 - The Digestive & Renal Systems** Read *T pp. 69-71* & Narrate Begin working on Fascinating Facts about the Digestive and Renal Systems *NJ pp. 52-53* Try This! *T p. 71* Read *T pp. 71-73* & Narrate Try This! *T p. 72*	Read *T pp. 74-77* & Narrate Try This! *T p. 76* Read *T pp. 77-80* & Narrate Try This! *T p. 78*
8	**Lesson 4 - The Digestive and Renal Systems** Read *T pp. 80-81* & Narrate Written Narration: What Do You Remember? *T p. 81, NJ p. 54* Notebooking Activity: Digestion Comic Strip *T p. 81, NJ p. 55*	Personal Person Project: Add the digestive and renal systems *T p. 82, NJ p. 15* Vocabulary Crosswords *NJ pp. 56-59* Scripture Copywork *NJ pp. 60-61* Digestion Minibook *NJ Appemdix p. A 15* Project: Design a Digestion Theme Park *T p. 82, NJ p. 64*

*Page numbers for the anatomy text are indicated by *T p.* Page numbers for the notebooking journal are indicated by *NJ p.*

Week	Day 1	Day 2
9	**Lesson 5 - Health and Nutrition** Read *T pp. 85-88* & Narrate Begin working on Fascinating Facts about Health and Nutrition *NJ p. 65* Try This! *T p. 87* Read *T pp. 88-89* & Narrate Try This! *T p. 89*	Read *T pp. 90-92* & Narrate Try This! *T p. 91* Try This! *T p. 92* Read *T pp. 93-95* & Narrate Try This! *T p. 93* Try This! *T p. 96* Try This! page to be used to record Try This! activities *NJ p. 67*
10	**Lesson 5 - Health and Nutrition** Read *T pp. 96-98* & Narrate Written Narration: What Do You Remember? *T p. 98, NJ p. 66* Project: Food Pyramid *T p. 99, NJ p. 68* Notebooking Activity: One-Week Dinner Menu *T p. 98, NJ p. 69-71*	Vocabulary Crosswords *NJ pp. 72-75* Scripture Copywork *NJ pp. 76-77* Nutrition Minibook *NJ Appendix p. A 21* Experiment: Testing for Vitamin C *T p. 99, NJ p. 81*
11	**Lesson 6 - The Respiratory System** Read *T pp. 103-106* & Narrate Begin working on Fascinating Facts About the Respiratory System *NJ pp. 82-83* Try This! *T p. 104* Try This! *T p. 105*	Read *T pp. 106-110* & Narrate Try This! *T p. 106* Try This! *T p. 108* Try This! *T p. 109* Try This! *T p. 110*
12	**Lesson 6 - The Respiratory System** Read *T pp. 111-115* & Narrate Try This! *T p. 114* Try This! *T p. 115* Written Narration: What Do You Remember? *T p. 116, NJ p. 84* Personal Person Project: Add a trachea, lungs and diaphragm *T p. 116, NJ p. 15*	Notebooking Activity: Write a Speech: The Dangers of Smoking *T p. 116, NJ p. 85* Vocabulary Crossword *NJ pp. 86-87* Scripture Copywork *NJ pp. 88-89* Respiratory Minibooks *NJ Appendix p. A 25* Experiment: Diaphragm Model *T p. 116* Experiment: Vital Lung Capacity *T p. 117*
13	**Lesson 7 - Life in the Blood** Read *T pp. 119-122* & Narrate Begin working on Fascinating Facts about Blood *NJ pp. 93-94* Try This! *T p. 122*	Read *T pp. 123-126* & Narrate Project: Blood Model *T p. 124* Try This! *T p. 127*
14	**Lesson 7 - Life in the Blood** Read *T pp. 127-131* & Narrate Written Narration: What Do You Remember? *T p. 131, NJ p. 95* Notebooking Activity: Blood Illustration *T p. 131, NJ p. 96*	Notebooking Activity: Write an Apologia *T p. 131, NJ p. 97* Vocabulary Crossword *NJ pp. 98-99* Scripture Copywork *NJ pp. 100-101* Blood Minibooks *NJ Appendix p. A 29* Experiment: Type Your Blood *T p. 132*
15	**Lesson 8 - The Cardiovascular System** Read *T pp. 133-135* & Narrate Begin working on Fascinating Facts about the Cardiovascular System *NJ pp. 105-106* Try This! *T p. 135* Read *T pp. 136-138* & Narrate Try This! *T p. 136* Try This! *T p. 137*	Read *T pp. 139-141* & Narrate Try This! *T p. 139* Try This! How Blood Flows Through the Heart *T p. 141, NJ p. 107* Read *T pp. 142-144* & Narrate Try This! *T p. 143*
16	**Lesson 8 - The Cardiovascular System** Read *T pp. 144-145* & Narrate Written Narration: What Do You Remember? *T p. 145, NJ p. 108* Notebooking Activity: Write an Advertisement *T p. 146, NJ p. 109*	Personal Person Project: Add a heart *T p. 146, NJ p. 15* Scripture Copywork *NJ pp. 110-111* Vocabulary Crossword *NJ pp. 112-113* Cardiovascular Minibooks *NJ Appendix p. A 33* Project: Make a Stethoscope *T p. 147, NJ p. 116*

*Page numbers for the anatomy text are indicated by *T p.* Page numbers for the notebooking journal are indicated by *NJ p.*

Week	Day 1	Day 2
17	**Lesson 9 - The Nervous and Endocrine Systems** Read *T pp. 149-152* & Narrate Begin working on Fascinating Facts about the Nervous and Endocrine Systems *NJ pp. 117-118* Try This! *T p. 151*	Read *T pp. 152-155* & Narrate Try This! *T p. 154* Read *T pp. 155-157* & Narrate Try This! *T pp. 156* Try This! *T pp. 157*
18	**Lesson 9 - The Nervous and Endocrine Systems** Read *T pp. 158-159* & Narrate Written Narration: What Do You Remember? *T p. 159, NJ pp. 119* Personal Person Project: Add a brain *T p. 159, NJ p. 15*	Notebooking Activity: Label a Brain and Neuron, Make a Venn Diagram *T p. 159, NJ pp. 120-121* Scripture Copywork *NJ pp. 122-123* Vocabulary Crosswords *NJ pp. 124-126* Nervous System Minibook *NJ Appendix p. A 37* Project: Anatomy Trivia Game *T p. 160, NJ p. 128*
19	**Lesson 10 - The Nervous System Extended** Read *T pp. 161-164* & Narrate Begin working on Fascinating Facts about the Nervous System Extended *NJ p. 130* Try This! *T p. 162* Try This! *T p. 164*	Read *T pp. 165-167* & Narrate Try This! *T p. 165* Try This! *T p. 166* Try This! *T p. 167* Read *T pp. 167-169* & Narrate Try This! *T p. 168*
20	**Lesson 10 - The Nervous System Extended** Read *T pp. 170-171* & Narrate Try This! *T p. 170* Written Narration: What Do You Remember? *T p. 172, NJ p. 131* Notebooking Activity: The Brain, Spinal Cord and Cerebral Lobes *T p. 172, NJ pp. 132-134*	Vocabulary Crossword *NJ p. 135* Scripture Copywork *NJ pp. 136-137* Brain Minibook *NJ Appendix p. A 41* Project: Design a Science Fair Project *T p. 172, NJ p. 140*
21	**Lesson 11 - Your Senses** Read T pp. 175-177 & Narrate Begin working on Fascinating Facts about Your Senses *NJ p. 141* Try This! *T p. 176* Try This! *T p. 177* Try This! *T p. 178* Read *T pp. 178-181* & Narrate Try This! *T p. 179* Try This! *T p. 180* Try This! *T p. 181*	Read *T pp. 182-185* & Narrate Try This! *T p. 182* Try This! *T p. 183* Try This! *T p. 185* Read *T pp. 186-188* & Narrate Try This! *T p. 186* Try This! *T p. 187* Try This! *T p. 188*
22	**Lesson 11 - Your Senses** Read *T pp. 189-191* & Narrate Try This! *T p. 189* Try This! *T p. 190* Written Narration: What Do You Remember? *T p. 191, NJ p. 142* Notebook Activity: Diagram of the Eye *T p. 191, NJ p. 143*	Vocabulary Crosswords *NJ pp. 144-147* Scripture Copywork *NJ pp. 148-149* Senses Minibook *NJ Appendix p. A 43* Experiment: Testing Taste *T p. 192*
23	**Lesson 12 - The Integumentary System** Read *T pp. 195-198* & Narrate Begin working on Fascinating Facts about the Integumentary System *NJ pp. 153-154* Read *T pp. 198-201* & Narrate Try This! *T p. 200*	Read *T pp. 202-204* & Narrate Try This! *T p. 202* Try This! *T p. 203* Try This! *T p. 204* Read *T pp. 205-207* & Narrate Try This! *T p. 206* Try This! *T p. 207*

*Page numbers for the anatomy text are indicated by *T p.* **Page numbers for the notebooking journal are indicated by** *NJ p.*

Week	Day 1	Day 2
24	**Lesson 12 - The Integumentary System** Read *T pp. 208-209* & Narrate Try This! *T p. 208* Written Narration: What Do You Remember? *T p. 209, NJ pp. 155* Personal Person Project: Add the skin *T p. 209, NJ p. 15* Notebooking Activity: Diagram of Skin *T p. 209, NJ p. 156*	Notebooking Activity: Fingerprints *T p. 209, NJ p. 157* Try This! pages to record Try This! activities *NJ p. 158, 161* Project: Braille Challenge *T p. 211, NJ p. 159* Scripture Copywork *NJ pp. 162-163* Vocabulary Crosswords *NJ pp. 164-165* Integumentary Minibook *NJ Appendix p. A 49* Experiment: Sensing Sensitivity *T p. 212, NJ p. 169*
25	**Lesson 13 - The Lymphatic and Immune Systems** Read *T pp. 215-218* & Narrate Begin working on Fascinating Facts about the Lymphatic and Immune Systems *NJ p. 170* Read *T pp. 219-221* & Narrate	Read *T pp. 221-224* & Narrate Read *T pp. 224-227* & Narrate
26	**Lesson 13 - The Lymphatic and Immune Systems** Written Narration: What Do You Remember? *T p. 227, NJ p. 171* Notebooking Activity: The Body's Defenses *T p. 227, NJ pp. 172-173*	Scripture Copywork *NJ pp. 174-175* Vocabulary Crosswords *NJ pp. 176-179* Defense Minibook *NJ Appendix p. A 53* Experiment: Testing for Bacteria and Fungi *T p. 228, NJ p. 183*
27	**Lesson 14 - Growth and Development** Read *T pp. 231-235* & Narrate Begin working on Fascinating Facts about Growth and Development and Human Beings *NJ p. 184* Try This! *T p. 233* Read *T pp. 235-238* & Narrate Try This! *T p. 236*	Read *T pp. 238-241* & Narrate Try This! *T p. 242* Read *T pp. 242-245* & Narrate
28	**Lesson 14 - Growth and Development** Read *T pp. 245-248* & Narrate Written Narration: What Do You Remember? *T p. 248, NJ p. 185* Notebooking Activity: Stages of Development *T p. 248, NJ p. 186* Notebooking Activity: Possible Purpose Page *T p. 248, NJ p. 187* Prayer Journal Activity *T p. 248*	Bible Reading Plan *T p. 249* Scripture Copywork *NJ pp. 188-189* Vocabulary Crossword *NJ pp. 190-191* Growth and Development Minibook *NJ Appendix p. A 55* Project: Dominant and Recessive Traits *T p. 250, NJ p. 194*

*Page numbers for the anatomy text are indicated by *T p.* Page numbers for the notebooking journal are indicated by *NJ p.*

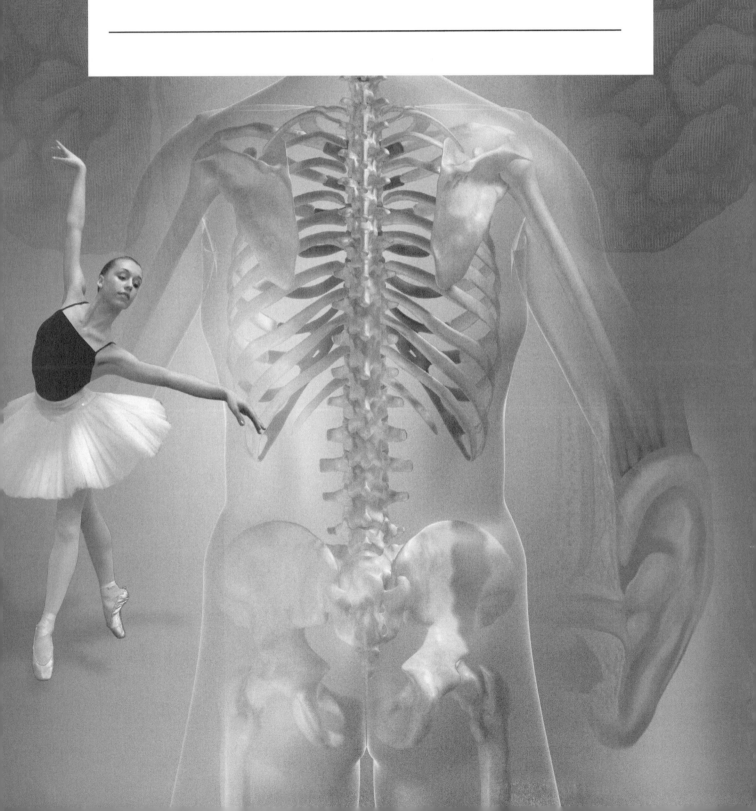

This journal belongs to:

_____

The instructions for creating your Personal Person can be found on page 12 of your anatomy textbook. The templates can be found on page A59 of this notebooking journal.

Fascinating Facts

about

Anatomy and Physiology

Lesson 1

Fascinating Facts

about

Anatomy and Physiology

Lesson 1

Cell Anatomy
Lesson 1

Cell Membrane **Mitochondria** **Golgi Body** **ER**

Ribosomes **Centrioles** **Lysosomes** **Nucleus**

NAME _____   DATE _____

WHAT DO YOU REMEMBER?
LESSON 1

1. What tells us that the Egyptians understood a lot about anatomy?

2. How do the laws that God gave to the Hebrews show us that God cares about our health?

3. What was wrong with the way the Greeks decided on their scientific beliefs?

4. What did Galen use to treat gladiators' wounds?

5. What did Hooke call the tiny rectangles he saw in the cork he examined under a microscope?

6. Name the different cell parts about which you've learned.

Egyptians

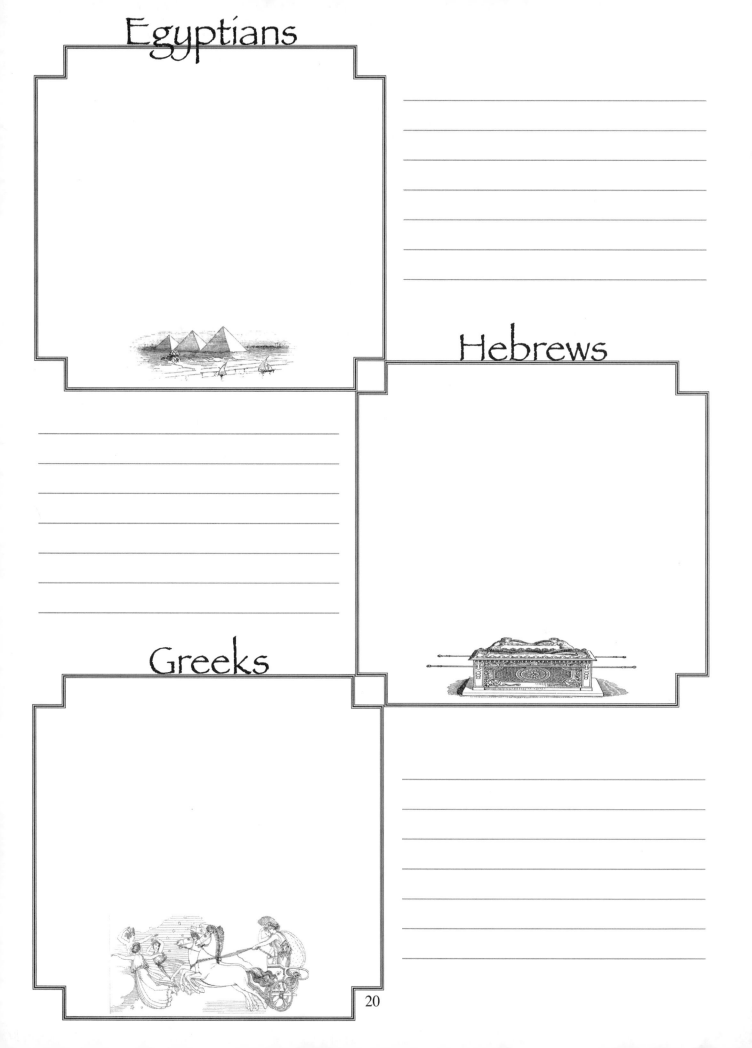

Hebrews

Greeks

Romans

Europeans

Microscope

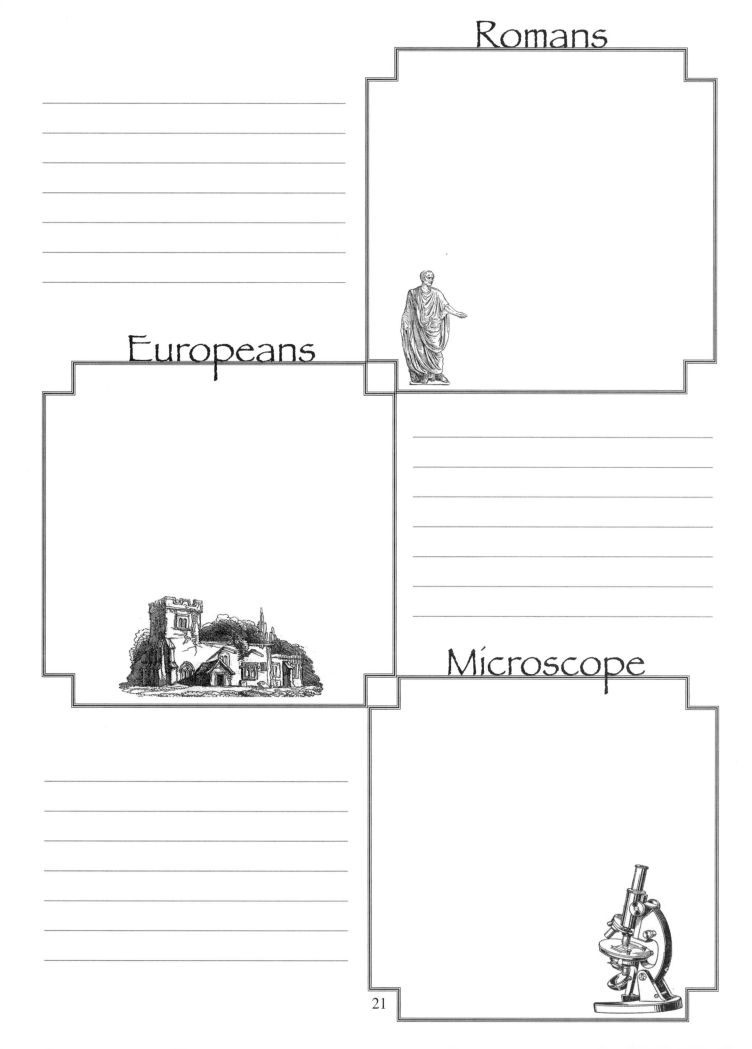

VOCABULARY CROSSWORD
ANATOMY AND PHYSIOLOGY

ANATOMY	HUMORS	CELL MEMBRANE	HIPPOCRATIC OATH
PHYSIOLOGY	PHLEGMATIC	ORGANELLES	ER
MUMMIES	SANGUINE	CYTOPLASM	CENTRIOLES
GERMS	CHOLERIC	MITOCHONDRIA	NUCLEUS
PARASITES	MELANCHOLY	GLUCOSE	NUCLEAR MEMBRANE
HYPOTHESIS	ARISTOTLE	LYSOSOMES	DNA
HIPPOCRATES	VESALIUS	GOLGI BODIES	NUCLEOTIDES
HOOKE	CADAVERS	TISSUE	CHROMOSOMES
RNA	DIFFERENTIATE	ORGAN	LEEUWENHOEK
SPONTANEOUS GENERATION			

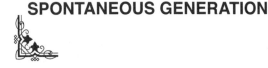

VOCABULARY CROSSWORD ANATOMY AND PHYSIOLOGY

Across

1. The jelly-like substance inside a cell, in which all the organelles float.
3. The study of the human body, all its parts, and how it's put together.
6. The organelles that look like stacked pancakes and store proteins and fats. TWO WORDS
8. A personality that is excitable and fully of energy.
10. An educated guess.
16. The scientist who used a microscope to examine cork, naming the little boxes he saw "cells."
18. A famous Greek philosopher that believed the body has four liquids that need to be balanced in order to be healthy.
19. A kind of sugar the cell uses.
21. The membrane that surrounds the nucleus. TWO WORDS
22. The control center of the cell.
27. Letters we use to refer to deoxyribonucleic acid, which is the molecule inside every living thing that contains all the information about that thing.
28. Small structures within a cell. The word means "little organs."
29. A personality that is easy to get along with and usually happy.
30. A Dutch scientist who discovered how to magnify things with glass lenses.
32. Dead bodies.
34. The name of the four liquids that Hippocrates believed would bring health to the body, if a person had equal amounts of the liquids.
35. The organelles inside a cell that give the cell power.

Down

2. A group of cells of the same type.
4. A group of tissues that work together to form a special body function.
5. DNA is packaged into units called_____. Your body has 46 of these units.
6. Tiny organisms that can cause diseases.
7. Organelles that protect the cell from foreign invaders and break down chemicals.
9. A Greek philosopher after Hippocrates, considered one of the greatest thinkers of all time.
11. The oath doctors take which states that they will always do good and never harm people. TWO WORDS
12. The wrong idea that life can come into existence from nonliving things. TWO WORDS.
13. What we call it when cells begin to become different from the original cell.
14. A personality that likes to be in control.
15. A French scientist who questioned Galen's ideas and dissected human cadavers.
17. Dead bodies that have been preserved using salt and chemicals to keep them from rotting and decaying.
20. The wall around a cell. TWO WORDS
21. These are strung together to make genes.
23. Tiny organisms (such as those sometimes found in pigs) that can infect humans and steal nutrients from the person they infect, as well as make the person sick.
24. A personality that is artistic and thoughtful.
25. The study of how all the parts of the body function.
26. Special organelles that help cells reproduce.
31. Two letters that we use to refer to the endoplasmic reticulum, which transports chemicals and gets rid of waste in a cell.
33. The DNA's messenger, which copies part of the information that is in the DNA and then leaves the nucleus.

Copywork

I will give thanks to You,
for I am fearfully and wonderfully made;
Wonderful are Your works,
And my soul knows it very well.

Psalm 139:14

Copywork

I will give thanks to You,
for I am fearfully and wonderfully made;
Wonderful are Your works,
And my soul knows it very well.

Psalm 139:14

Cell Minibook
Lesson 1

Paste your Cell Wheel
onto this page.

Be a Modern Vesalius

Vesalius drew the human body quite accurately. Using images found on page 32 of your textbook, try to draw the internal organs of a human body to scale. Also, Vesalius built prosthetics that are still used as models today. Using different materials attempt to build a prosthetic leg or arm that bends with the use of a pulley and strings. You can use materials such as: funnels, cardboard tubes, strings, metal fasteners, plastic rings, cardboard, tape and glue.

Experiment with a Magnifying Glass or Microscope

It's fascinating to view things up close. Use a magnifying glass or microscope to get a better look at your anatomy! Try looking at your skin, hair, fingernails, teeth, eyes, or nose. It would also be interesting to see a scab or open wound up close. Are you surprised by what you see?

Choosy Cell

The cell membrane is selectively permeable and very choosy about what it lets in and out of the cell. Let's see how it works! Put a few tablespoons of corn starch in a plastic sandwich bag and tie or zip the top. Next, immerse the bag in a glass of water with enough iodine to make the water dark golden brown. Now, let the bag sit for a couple of days. What do you think will happen? The baking soda will turn brown from the iodine seeping into the bag, but there will be no water inside the bag. Why? The "pores" of the bag are too small to allow water molecules through but are large enough to let the smaller iodine molecules through. The bag acts like a cell membrane, allowing some things in but keeping other things out.

Book and DVD Suggestions

The History of Medicine by John Hudson Tiner. This is a wonderful, well written book on the history of anatomy. It's a must read for everyone and is sure to become a family favorite!

Enjoy Your Cells by Fran Balkwill & Mic Rolph. This book does a great job of teaching about cells, though it does not cover the specific functions of the organelles within the cells. That will be covered well in the first lesson of *Exploring Creation with Human Anatomy and Physiology*.

Galen and the Gateway to Medicine by Jeanne Bendick. This fascinating biography brings Galen's Roman world alive! It helps the reader understand the medical knowledge and practices of that time period. The maps, diagrams and charts are helpful additions to the text. Recommended for ages 10 and up.

Magic School Bus: The Human Body. This DVD explores the human body. You may need to remind your children that lying is wrong as one child continually lies in the video.

Cell-a-bration Cytology: Newton's Workshop. Learn about cells with this live action DVD as Grandpa Newton and the kids explore God's creation with an old microscope. (Ages 7-12) 60 minutes.

DNA Decoders: Newton's Workshop. Learn about DNA with this live action DVD. (Ages 7-12) 60 minutes.

My Anatomy Projects
Lesson 1

What I did:

What I did:

What I learned:

What I learned:

Fascinating Facts

about the

SKELETAL SYSTEM

LESSON 2

WHAT DO YOU REMEMBER?
LESSON 2

1. Name the different things that bones do for your body.

2. What is the periosteum?

3. What mineral makes compact bone strong and hard?

4. What is the bone tissue that forms tunnels and pores called?

5. What are the two kinds of bone marrow?

6. What are osteoblasts?

7. Where are the smallest bones in your body found?

8. Which is the longest bone in your body?

9. What do ligaments do?

10. What is the rounded part of your skull called?

11. Can you name at least five other bones in your body by their scientific names?

12. Can you name at least one kind of joint?

SKELETON
LESSON 2

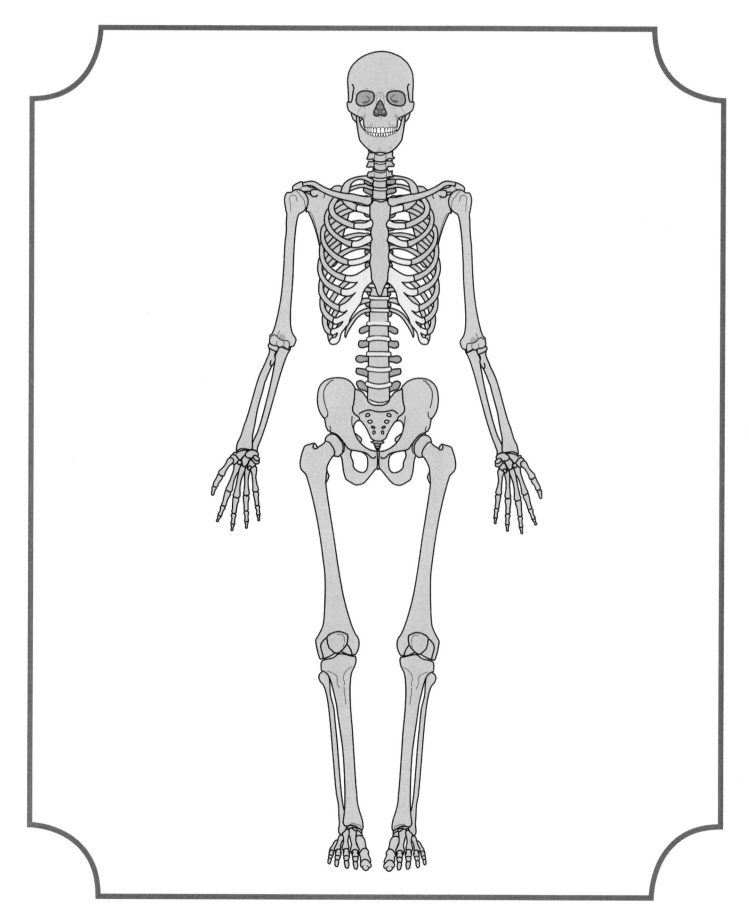

VOCABULARY CROSSWORD
SKELETAL SYSTEM

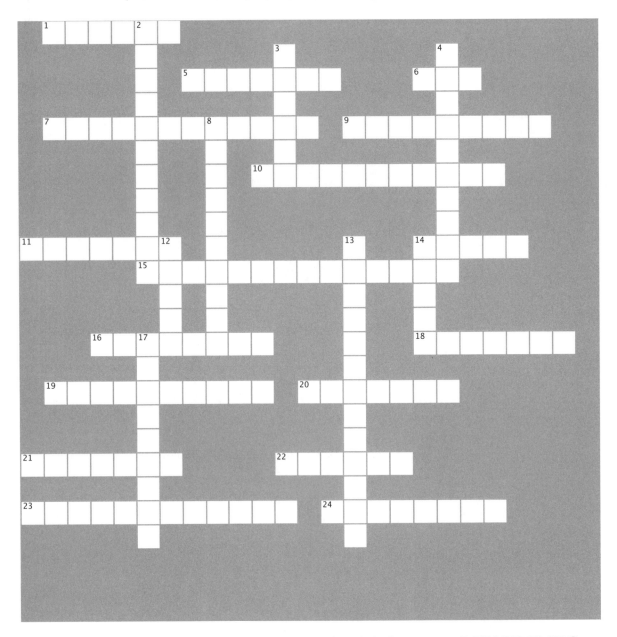

SKELETAL SYSTEM
SKULL
RIB CAGE
LIPIDS
CALCIUM
SUTURES
CALLUS
YELLOW
OSTEOCLASTS

OSTEOPOROSIS
VITAMIN D
RICKETS
MALNUTRITION
PERIOSTEUM
SYNOVIAL FLUID
FUSED
RED

REMODELING
COLLAGEN
SPONGY BONE
LIGAMENTS
CRANIUM
FEMUR
OSTEOBLASTS
CARTILAGE

VOCABULARY CROSSWORD
SKELETAL SYSTEM

Across

1. This is the kind of bone marrow in which lipids (fats) are stored.
5. A mineral stored in your bones that helps keep your heart beating and your brain thinking. It also makes your bones strong.
6. This is the kind of bone marrow in which blood cells are made.
7. A disease that results in weak bones with lots of tiny holes in them.
9. A firm but resilient material in the body and on the ends of bones that absorbs shock well and keeps the bones from getting hurt when they rub against one another.
10. The bone cells that eat away at the spongy layer, causing your bones to get wider.
11. A disease that causes weak and misformed bones. People can get this disease when they do not get enough vitamin D.
14. This is what occurs when two smaller bones are joined together to form one bone.
15. The bony supportive structure within the human body. TWO WORDS
16. The tough fiber that makes up part of the bone.
18. The bones that protect your heart and lungs. TWO WORDS
19. The layer of bone under the compact bone. It is a network of pores and tunnels interconnected in a pattern that makes the bone strong yet resilient. TWO WORDS
20. The bones of your skull that protect your brain.
21. Joints that do not move.
22. A bulge that occurs in a broken bone while it is healing.
23. When a person doesn't get enough of the right kinds of nutrients.
24. Your body needs _____ to make strong bones. Your body makes this when it is exposed to the sun. TWO WORDS

Down

2. The cells that make new bones.
3. Fats that are stored in your bones, as well as elsewhere in your body.
4. The outside layer of a bone: a thin, tough membrane.
8. What scientists call it when the body breaks down old bone and rebuilds new bone.
12. The group of bones that make up your head.
13. Fluid that allows the joints to move more easily. TWO WORDS
14. The longest bone in the body – the thigh bone.
17. The tissues that connect one bone to another bone.

Copywork

And the LORD will continually guide you, And satisfy your desire in scorched places, And give strength to your bones.

Isaiah 58:11

Copywork

And the LORD will continually guide you, And satisfy your desire in scorched places, And give strength to your bones.

Isaiah 58:11

BONES MINIBOOK
LESSON 2

Paste your Skeletal System
Shutter Book onto this page.

LESSON 2

Do a Word Study

What does the Bible say about bones? Use a concordance to find out! Look up the words "bone" and "bones" to see all the verses that contain these two words. Do a word study by looking up the verses. Write down your findings and present what the Bible says about bones to your family.

Reconstruct a Skeleton

Find a large picture of a skeleton and study the locations of the bones. Cut out each bone from the skeleton, then see if you can reconstruct the skeleton without looking at a model.

Test the Bone Strength of Different Animals

Over the course of a few weeks, save any bones from the different meals your family eats. Try to get an assortment of bones from different kinds of animals: cows, chickens, pigs and fish.

Now make a guess about which animal you think has the strongest bones. Test all the bones by submerging them in vinegar for two weeks to find out which ones break down the quickest. Check the bones every day, noting which ones are becoming soft and pliable. After two weeks in the vinegar, which animal's bones remained strong and sturdy? Was your original guess correct?

Examine X rays

X rays were discovered because of how radiation changed photo paper. Do some fun experiments with photosensitive paper. You can either get a Photo Print Kit (I saw some on eBay) or buy some paper from a supplier. Alternately, you can make photosensitive paper yourself using ferric ammonium citrate (be sure to discard it properly as it can contaminate the environment).

Bones for Dinner?

Did you know that bones are full of nutrition? It's true! People used to eat bone marrow for its nutritional value. It was even considered a delicacy! Chicken bones were also used in soups because of the minerals they provide. You can do an Internet search to find other ways in which people enjoyed the nutritional value of bones! Yum!

Book Suggestion

Roentgen: The Head Bone's Connected to the Neck Bone by McClafferty. I personally read and enjoyed this book.

DVD Suggestion

Standard Deviants School - Anatomy, Program 1 - Bones (Classroom Edition). This fast paced, action packed DVD takes you on an exciting journey into the skeletal system.

My Bones Projects
Lesson 2

What I did:

What I did:

What I learned:

What I learned:

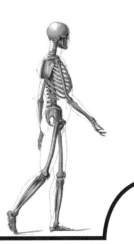

SCIENTIFIC SPECULATION SHEET

Analyzing a Chicken Bone
Lesson 2

Name_____   Date _____

Materials Used:

Procedure:

Hypothesis:

Results:

Conclusion:

Fascinating Facts

about the

MUSCULAR SYSTEM

LESSON 3

Fascinating Facts

about the

MUSCULAR SYSTEM

LESSON 3

_____
_____
_____
_____
_____
_____
_____
_____
_____
_____
_____
_____
_____
_____
_____

_____
_____
_____
_____
_____
_____

WHAT DO YOU REMEMBER?
LESSON 3

1. What are the three kinds of muscle tissue in your body?

2. Which of those muscle kinds are voluntary, and which are involuntary?

3. What is muscle tone?

4. What are tendons?

5. Where is your Achilles tendon?

6. What are antagonistic muscles?

7. What do muscle cells have a lot of that give them energy?

8. What substances help muscles move?

9. What do muscles need to grow?

10. How do you keep your cardiac muscle strong?

11. Name two places in your body where you find smooth muscles.

MUSCLE TIMES

VOCABULARY CROSSWORD
MUSCULAR SYSTEM

SKELETAL MUSCLES
LACTIC ACID
RAPID EYE MOVEMENT
EXTENSOR MUSCLES
REFLEXIVE
ACHILLES TENDON
ANTAGONISTIC MUSCLES

CARDIAC MUSCLE
GLUTEUS MAXIMUS
VOLUNTARY MUSCLES
TENDONITIS
ANAEROBIC
MASSETER
ATROPHY

FILAMENTS
GLUCOSE
MYOFIBRILS
FLEXOR MUSCLES
MUSCLE TONE
TENDONS
AEROBIC

VOCABULARY CROSSWORD MUSCULAR SYSTEM

Across

6. The muscle that connects to the back of the pelvic girdle and femur. TWO WORDS
9. The way the eye moves during sleep. THREE WORDS
14. This is another name for skeletal muscles, because you can control them by thinking about controlling them. TWO WORDS
16. Muscles that close the joints. TWO WORDS
18. A cellular waste product created when energy is produced anaerobically. TWO WORDS
19. Muscles that open the joints wider. TWO WORDS
20. The type of energy production that requires oxygen.
21. The tendon that attaches the calf muscle to the heel bone. TWO WORDS

Down

1. The type of cellular energy generation that occurs when there is an inadequate supply of oxygen in that cell.
2. A condition that occurs when a muscle is underused and therefore becomes weak and shrinks.
3. The small strips of protein located inside each myofibril.
4. The muscles that are attached to and move your bones. TWO WORDS
5. The muscle that closes the mouth and keeps it closed.
7. A pair of muscles or muscle groups that act to pull a bone in opposite directions. TWO WORDS
8. This condition occurs when tendons are overused and become inflamed.
10. The muscle type that forms much of the heart. TWO WORDS
11. A sugar that the human body turns certain foods into. It can be used to make energy to power muscle cells.
12. These connect skeletal muscles to bones.
13. The type of action whereby muscles move involuntarily.
15. This is produced when muscles are partially contracted. TWO WORDS
17. Strands of protein inside skeletal muscle cells.

Copywork

The LORD is my strength and my
song; he has become my salvation.
Exodus 15:2

Copywork

The LORD is my strength and my song; he has become my salvation.

Exodus 15:2

MUSCLES MINIBOOK
LESSON 3

Paste your Muscular
System Flap Book onto
this page.

Bible Study on Strength

Our muscles give us strength. What does the Bible say about strength? Use a concordance to find out! Look up the word "strength" to see all the verses that contain this word. Do a word study by looking up the verses. Write down your findings. Also, write down any area in which you feel you need God's strength, then ask God to strengthen you in this area. Encourage your family by presenting what the Bible says about strength.

Book Suggestions

Muscles: Our Muscular System by Seymour Simons. This book is highly ranked and contains beautiful illustrations and great content concerning the different muscle groups. Be aware that it may contain teachings on evolution.

Understanding Your Muscles and Bones by Usborne Books. Using lively text, colorful diagrams and comical illustrations, this book takes children "under the skin" to see how muscles and bones work.

DVD Suggestions

Human Body: Pushing the Limits Disc 1. Although overly focused on evolution, this DVD on muscle strength and the amazing design and abilities of the human body is extremely well done. If you choose to watch this DVD, keep in mind that there is no evidence for evolution. Rather, it is our great God who designed the intricacies of the human body.

Standard Deviants School - Anatomy, Program 2 - Muscles (Classroom Edition). This fast paced, action packed DVD takes you on an exciting journey into the muscular system.

My Muscles Projects
Lesson 3

What I did:

What I did:

What I learned:

What I learned:

SCIENTIFIC SPECULATION SHEET

Growing Muscle

Lesson 3

Name_____   Date _____

Materials Used:

Procedure:

Hypothesis:

Results:

Conclusion:

Fascinating Facts

about the

DIGESTIVE SYSTEM

LESSON 4

Fascinating Facts

about the

DIGESTIVE SYSTEM

Lesson 4

53

WHAT DO YOU REMEMBER?
LESSON 4

1. What is the white outer layer of your tooth called?

2. What is the layer right below that called?

3. What is the hardest substance in your body?

4. Name a few things saliva does for you.

5. What is the name of the pipe that food goes down after you swallow it?

6. How do you keep from getting burned by your own stomach acid?

7. What is the food called when it enters the small intestine?

8. What happens in the small intestine?

9. Which organ is like a huge chemical factory?

10. What do the kidneys do?

Digestion Comic

VOCABULARY CROSSWORD
DIGESTIVE SYSTEM

DIGESTION

EPIGLOTTIS

PREMOLARS

SALIVA

DEFECATION

ENAMEL

LARYNX

PULP

CROWN

ENZYMES

DENTIN

CHEMICAL DIGESTION

ALIMENTARY CANAL

INCISORS

MECHANICAL DIGESTION

CUSPIDS

MOLARS

VOCABULARY CROSSWORD
DIGESTIVE SYSTEM

Across

4. Chemicals that, among other things, help your body break food down into smaller components.
5. Teeth in the back of your mouth that are useful for grinding food.
11. The part of digestion which involves the grinding and moving along of food through the digestive canal. TWO WORDS
13. The teeth located in front of your molars. They are useful for grinding food.
14. Sometimes called your canines, these teeth are sharp and are made for tearing food.
16. The part of the tooth not hidden by the gums. It is covered with enamel.
17. The passage that leads to the lungs, located right in front of the entrance to the esophagus.

Down

1. The extremely hard, white, shiny substance that coats your teeth.
2. The process of digestion where the chemicals in foods are changed into smaller chemical components so your body can use them. TWO WORDS
3. The last step in digestion; the elimination of solid waste from the alimentary canal.
6. The part of the digestive system through which food passes, also called the gastrointestinal tract. TWO WORDS
7. A flap of cartilage in the back of your throat that drops down over the larynx and prevents food from going down the larynx.
8. The body's process of breaking down food and converting it into the material the body needs to live, repair itself, and grow.
9. The front four teeth, which are sharp and useful for biting.
10. The area below the enamel and dentin, which contains the nerves and blood vessels.
12. The living substance under the enamel on your tooth that supports it and absorbs shock that could otherwise damage the tooth.
15. A liquid produced by the salivary glands (which are located in and near the mouth), containing enzymes that begin the breakdown of starches.

VOCABULARY CROSSWORD
DIGESTIVE AND RENAL SYSTEMS

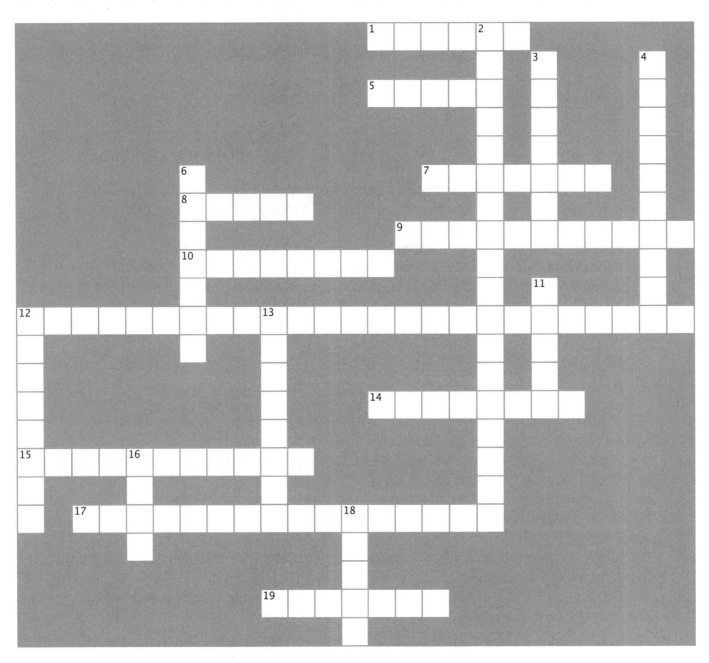

PEPSIN
BLADDER
JEJUNUM
APPENDIX
ILEUM
URETERS
VILLI

GLYCOGEN
DUODENUM
PANCREAS
RENAL SYSTEM
FLATULENCE
GALL BLADDER
PYLORIC SPHINCTER

LIVER
CHYME
BILE
KIDNEYS
ILEOCECAL SPHINCTER
GASTROESOPHAGEAL SPHINCTER

VOCABULARY CROSSWORD
DIGESTIVE AND RENAL SYSTEMS

Across

1. A powerful enzyme in the stomach that is needed to break down the proteins eaten into smaller chemical components that the body can use.
5. The liquid substance food becomes after being broken down in the stomach.
7. Urine trickles down these tubes.
8. The part of the body where nutrients are processed.
9. The place in your body where urine is produced. TWO WORDS
10. The first foot-long part of the intestine.
12. A circular muscle at the meeting point between the esophagus and the stomach. TWO WORDS
14. A tube on the cecum that provides a place for bacteria to live until needed.
15. The part of the body that releases concentrated bile into the duodenum. TWO WORDS
17. A muscle that works carefully to ensure that only a small amount of chyme goes into the small intestine at a time. TWO WORDS
19. The eight-foot long part of the intestine, after the duodenum.

Down

2. The meeting point between the small and large intestines that opens and closes to let the liquid chyme from the small intestine enter the large intestine. TWO WORDS
3. Special organs in your renal system that produce urine.
4. A side effect that occurs when bacteria in your intestines digest carbohydrates and release different gases.
6. The ureters lead down to this pouch.
11. Tiny projections inside the small intestine that help transport nutrients to blood vessels throughout the intestine.
12. Glucose molecules made by the liver from extra glucose in the body.
13. An organ used for digestion that produces hormones as well as digestive juices.
16. One of the chemicals made by the liver that is important for the digestive process.
18. The last eleven feet of the small intestine.

Copywork

I am the LORD your God, who
brought you up out of Egypt. Open
wide your mouth and I will fill it.

Psalm 81:10

Copywork

I am the LORD your God, who brought you up out of Egypt. Open wide your mouth and I will fill it.

Psalm 81:10

DIGESTION MINIBOOK
LESSON 4

Paste your Digestion
Pocket onto this page.

Antacid Experiment

Using hydrochloric acid, which is very similar to stomach acid, you can test which antacids work best to reduce acid indigestion. You will need to dissolve several different antacids (with the same milligram content) in warm water. Fill several beakers with the same amount of hydrochloric acid. Test each beaker with a different antacid, determining which one worked more quickly and effectively to neutralize the acid.

How do Enzymes Work?

A special enzyme called Papain is found in meat tenderizers. Let's do an experiment to see how this enzyme affects meat.

You will need:
1/4 cup of lunch meat
1 tsp of meat tenderizer
2 small jars with lids
Water

Put half of the meat in one jar. Add enough water to cover the meat. Put the lid on the jar and label it "water." Put the rest of the meat in the other jar. Cover it with the same amount of water. Add one teaspoon of meat tenderizer to the water. Put the lid on the jar and label it "Papain." Observe the jars for two days and record what you learn.

Digestion Differences

Do some research to learn about the different kinds of animal digestion. Be sure to study the digestion of ruminating animals, such as cows and deer, and also some unusual digestive habits of animals such as rabbits. Do a comparison and contrast between humans and these animals.

Book Suggestions

Disgusting Digestion by Nick Arnold. This book is written in a funny style, detailing lots of facts and information about digestion and the history of medicine as it relates to the topic.

What Happens to Your Food by Usborne Books. Watch how your food slips and slides through your body with this amazing book! Lift the flaps to find out what happens inside when you eat.

Why do People Eat? by Usborne Books. The simple text and detailed illustrations combine to answer questions related to why people eat. Answers are presented in clear, step-by-step stages and provide a wealth of information for the young reader.

My Digestion Projects
Lesson 4

What I did:

What I did:

What I learned:

What I learned:

Fascinating Facts
about
NUTRITION
LESSON 5

WHAT DO YOU REMEMBER?
LESSON 5

1. How do you know if you are dehydrated?

2. Why do simple carbohydrates give you quick bursts of energy, while complex carbohydrates don't necessarily do that?

3. What do carbohydrates change into inside the body?

4. Proteins are made of what kind of molecules strung together?

5. What is a complete protein?

6. Which foods provide your body with omega 3 fatty acids?

7. Name three vitamins that are important to get, and tell why they are important.

8. Where are minerals found?

9. Name two minerals, and tell why they are important for your body.

TRY THIS!

What I did:

What I did:

What I learned:

What I learned:

FOOD PYRAMID

LESSON 5

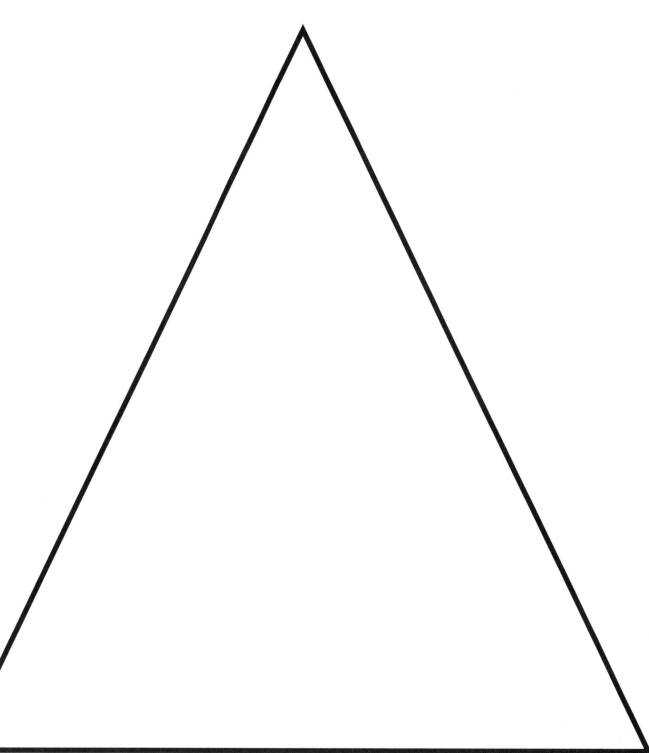

My Menus

Here you will make a pocket in which to keep all your menus. Cut a sheet of construction paper in half and glue it over this text along the bottom and side edges of the rectangle. Do not glue down the top edge! Make copies of the menu template on the previous page, or go to the book extras page I told you about at the beginning of this book to download a copy you can print from your printer. You can also create your own menu templates. Be sure to save all your menus in this pocket. You'll want to refer to them for future meals!

VOCABULARY CROSSWORD HEALTH AND NUTRITION

NUTRIENTS
MOLECULES
FRUCTOSE
GLUCOSE
GLYCOGEN
FATTY ACIDS
OMEGA 6
TRANS FATS
GLYCEROL

ATOMS
CARBOHYDRATES
GLYCEMIC INDEX
BLOOD SUGAR
PROTEIN
OMEGA 3
HYDROGENATION
CALORIES

SIMPLE CARBOHYDRATES
COMPLEX CARBOHYDRATES
ESSENTIAL AMINO ACIDS
ESSENTIAL FATTY ACIDS
UNSATURATED FATS
INCOMPLETE PROTEIN
COMPLETE PROTEIN
SATURATED FATS
TRIGLYCERIDES

VOCABULARY CROSSWORD
HEALTH AND NUTRITION

Across

2. A strand of amino acids; a substance made and used in every cell in your body.
7. A process whereby unsaturated fats are chemically converted into saturated fats.
12. Your body turns most carbohydrates into this one simple carbohydrate.
17. The nine amino acids that your body cannot make, but that are essential (required) for your cells to make the proteins they need. THREE WORDS
19. Small carbohydrate molecules (sugars) that digest easily and provide "quick energy" for your body. TWO WORDS
21. Units we use to measure energy.
22. Substances found in food and drink that your body needs to be healthy.
23. The smallest units of an element that retain the properties of the element.
24. Carbon, hydrogen and oxygen atoms linked together in specific forms that can be broken down to give your body the energy it needs.
25. Three fatty acid molecules are linked together with this molecule to form a fat.

Down

1. The liver changes glucose into this complex carbohydrate. It becomes stored energy for later use.
3. The type of essential fatty acid of which your body needs the greatest amount. It is found in most cooking oils. TWO WORDS
4. Unhealthy fats that have been industrially altered through hydrogenation. TWO WORDS
5. Large carbohydrate molecules (unrefined starches) that take a long time to digest. They release energy into your bloodstream slowly. TWO WORDS
6. The measure for how quickly food releases energy (in the form of glucose) into your bloodstream. TWO WORDS
8. The fatty acids your body can't make but must have in order to continue making the special fats it needs to survive. THREE WORDS
9. The very sweet sugar found in most fruits.
10. A protein (like those found in vegetables) that contains only some of the essential amino acids. TWO WORDS
11. A protein, such as those from meat or eggs, that contains all nine essential amino acids. TWO WORDS
13. These are formed when two or more different kinds of atoms are linked together.
14. Fats are made up of three _____ attached to a glycerol. TWO WORDS
15. Fats that are usually liquid at room temperature, such as those that come from olives or nuts. TWO WORDS
16. Another name for fats, based on the three fatty acid chains linked to a glycerol to make a fat.
18. One of the two types of essential fatty acids your body needs. Among other foods, it can be found in tuna, dark leafy green vegetables and flax seeds. TWO WORDS
19. Fats that are usually solid at room temperature, such as butter. TWO WORDS
20. What we call the glucose in your bloodstream. TWO WORDS

VOCABULARY CROSSWORD
VITAMINS

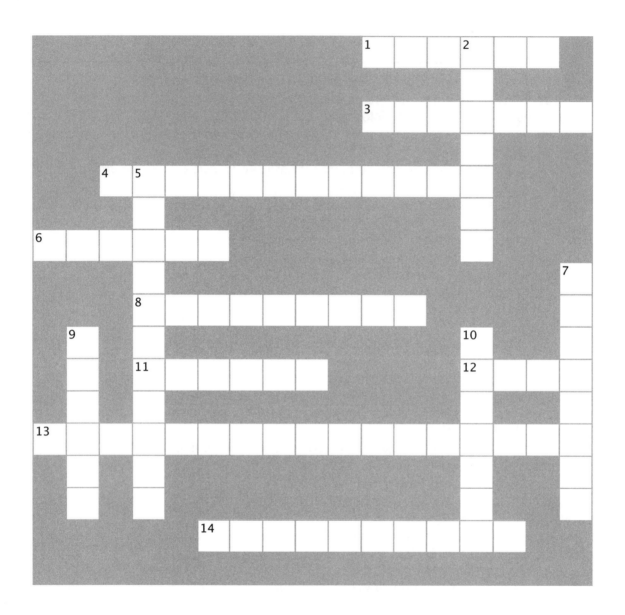

VITAMIN DEFICIENCY
IODINE
GOITER
FAT SOLUBLE
IRON
SCURVY
OXIDATION

WATER SOLUBLE
SODIUM
ANTIOXIDANT
CALCIUM
RICKETS
MINERAL
COENZYME

VOCABULARY CROSSWORD
VITAMINS

Across

1. A disease caused by a vitamin C deficiency.
3. A mineral your body needs to have strong bones.
4. A vitamin that dissolves easily in water and is not stored in your body is said to be _____. TWO WORDS
6. A swelling of the thyroid gland that can result from a lack of iodine.
8. What occurs when fruits are exposed to air, and the oxygen stimulates cellular enzymes to begin to break down the cell walls, turning the fruit brown.
11. A mineral found in seawater and iodized salt.
12. An important mineral for your body that is plentiful in beef.
13. A condition that occurs when your body doesn't get the proper amount of a vitamin it needs. TWO WORDS
14. A vitamin that dissolves easily in fat and is stored in your body is said to be _____. TWO WORDS

Down

2. A disease caused by a vitamin D deficiency, affecting how bones grow and remodel.
5. Something that helps to stop the oxidation process.
7. An enzyme's helper. Some vitamins play this helper role in your body.
9. One of the minerals that your body needs most. It is found in table salt.
10. A nutrient originally obtained from non-living sources. These nutrients are usually found in the earth, rivers, lakes, streams and oceans, and many are required by your body.

Copywork

Do not be wise in your own eyes; fear the LORD and shun evil. This will bring health to your body and nourishment to your bones.

Proverbs 3:7-8

Copywork

Do not be wise in your own eyes; fear the LORD and shun evil. This will bring health to your body and nourishment to your bones.

Proverbs 3:7 -8

NUTRITION MINIBOOK
LESSON 5

Paste your Nutrition
Matchbook onto this
page.

The Bible and Food

What does the Bible say about foods that are good for you? Read the story of Daniel and learn about the food he ate when he was taken into captivity. You can also study the different foods mentioned in the Bible. Which foods are considered healthy and which are considered unhealthy? Why did God deem some clean and some unclean? Organize your findings into a report and present it to your family.

People in the Bible grew their own food. Did it taste better than the store bought food we eat today? You can find out by growing some fruits and vegetables in your back yard. Do a taste test by comparing your homegrown food with the same food items from a grocery store. Which do your taste buds prefer: store bought or homegrown?

Vitamin C and Cold Prevention

Vitamin C is said to be effective against colds. Conduct an experiment to see whether taking vitamin C can prevent or lesson the symptoms associated with the common cold. Gather a large group of people. Instruct half of the group to take vitamin C every day for 30 days, and the other half not to take any vitamin C. Contact the people regularly during the 30 day period to see if they have experienced any cold symptoms. Note the severity of the symptoms. At the end of the 30 days, compare the two groups. Write a summary of your findings about the effectiveness of vitamin C for cold prevention. If done correctly, this could be a great science fair project.

Plants and Vitamins

The nutrients we feed plants are like vitamins for the plants. You can conduct an experiment to identify which brand of food is best for plants. You can also experiment to find out which types of nutrients are best for plants. You will need three identical plants in identical soil and containers, placed in the same spot and watered the exact same amount. You will also need two kinds of plant food. One of the three plants will be your control plant, receiving no food at all. The other two should be tested with one kind of plant food each. After a time, measure the plants' growth and color (inductive and deductive data) and record which plant fared best.

Cookbooks for Kids

The Gastrokid Cookbook by Hugh Garvey and Matthew Yeomans. This cookbook is for the kid who's willing to boldly explore new culinary tastes and experiences!

New Junior Cookbook: Better Homes and Gardens. The adult version of this "red and white checked" cookbook was the staple of my parents' kitchen and is a staple in mine as well.

Southern Living Kids Cookbook by Southern Living. This cookbook contains 124 recipes that kids will love to cook and eat!

"C" is for Cooking: Recipes from the Street by Susan McQuillan. Every recipe in this cookbook highlights at least one task that a young child can perform.

My Nutrition Projects
Lesson 5

What I did:

What I did:

What I learned:

What I learned:

SCIENTIFIC SPECULATION SHEET

Testing for Vitamin C

Lesson 5

Name_____   Date _____

Materials Used:

Procedure:

Hypothesis:

Results:

Conclusion:

Fascinating Facts

about the

RESPIRATORY SYSTEM

LESSON 6

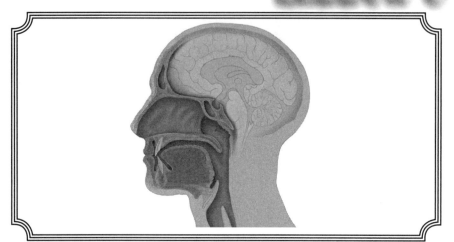

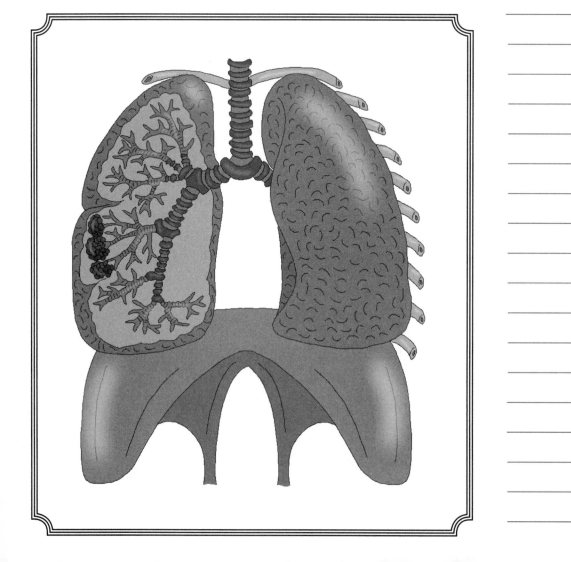

Fascinating Facts

about the

RESPIRATORY SYSTEM

LESSON 6

The Breathing Process

WHAT DO YOU REMEMBER?
LESSON 6

1. What does the hair in your nose do?

2. What does the mucus in your nasal passage do?

3. What are cilia?

4. Explain how the conchae help to warm and moisten the air you breathe.

5. What are the thin strips of tissue in your larynx called?

6. What determines your voice's pitch?

7. What determines your voice's volume?

8. How do the cartilage rings around your trachea help you?

9. What are your bronchi?

10. Explain the importance of alveoli.

11. Name some of the dangers of smoking.

12. How does the oxygen get from your lungs into your blood?

13. What muscle is mostly responsible for your breathing?

SMOKING SPEECH

_____
_____
_____
_____
_____
_____
_____
_____
_____
_____
_____
_____
_____
_____
_____
_____
_____
_____
_____
_____
_____
_____
_____
_____
_____
_____
_____
_____
_____

VOCABULARY CROSSWORD
RESPIRATORY SYSTEM

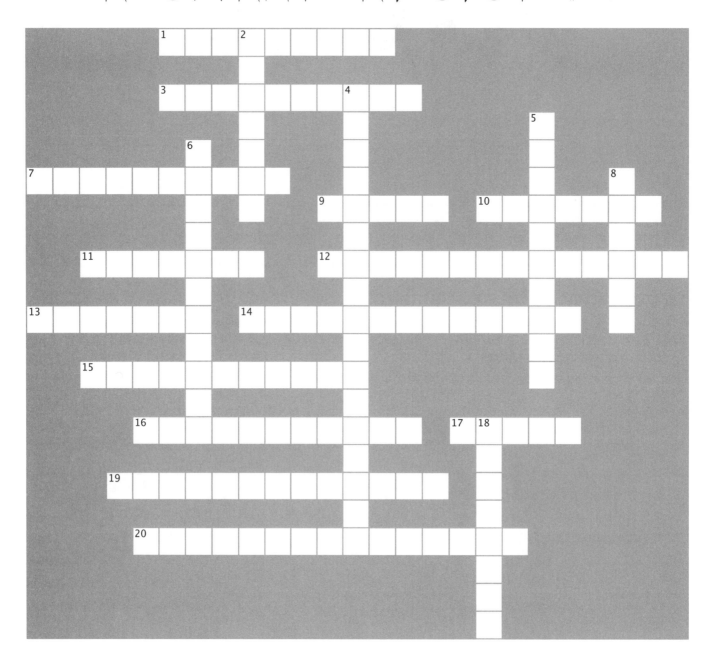

NASAL CAVITY
CILIA
SINUS CAVITIES
UVULA
VOICE BOX
BRONCHI
ALVEOLAR DUCTS

DIAPHRAGM
CONCHAE
PHARYNX
OROPHARYNX
LARYNX
BRONCHITIS
ALVEOLI

RESPIRATORY SYSTEM
MUCOUS MEMBRANES
NASOPHARYNX
LARYNGOPHARYNX
VOCAL CORDS
BRONCHIOLES

VOCABULARY CROSSWORD RESPIRATORY SYSTEM

Across

1. The long muscle below your lungs. It helps you breathe in and out.
3. "Strings" or strips of tissue that are pulled tightly across your larynx. They vibrate as air blows by, giving you the ability to make sounds. TWO WORDS
7. The part of the pharynx that is closest to your mouth.
9. Tiny motorized "whips" waving back and forth on the cells lining the back of your nose and throughout much of the respiratory tract.
10. Air passes through these structures in your nasal cavity where it is cleaned, moistened and brought to the correct temperature.
11. The two tubes that branch out from the trachea.
12. The last part of the pharynx.
13. Balloon-like sacs in the lungs that allow the oxygen you need to pass easily from the air you inhale into the blood stream.
14. Bronchioles fan out to create these little spaces where air enters the alveoli. TWO WORDS
15. A space in your head where much of the dust, pollen, bacteria and other stuff in the air you breathe is filtered out. TWO WORDS
16. The uppermost part of the pharynx. It is connected to the inner ear.
17. A small pink projection hanging downward from your soft palate.
19. Holes in your skull that aid in the warming, moisturizing and filtering of the air you breathe. TWO WORDS
20. Mucus producing tissues, found in many parts of your body. TWO WORDS

Down

2. Air passes through the three parts of this structure on its way down to the trachea.
4. The system that enables you to breathe; your nose, trachea, and lungs are a few of the parts of this system. TWO WORDS
5. The condition that occurs when your bronchi are swollen, usually because of an infection.
6. Very small, thin-walled tubes that carry air to where the lungs can finally use it.
8. The part of your body that gives you the ability to speak.
18. Another name for the larynx. TWO WORDS

Copywork

Then the LORD God formed man of dust from the ground, and breathed into his nostrils the breath of life; and man became a living being.

Genesis 2:7

_____

_____

_____

_____

_____

_____

Copywork

Then the LORD God formed man of dust from the ground, and breathed into his nostrils the breath of life; and man became a living being.

Genesis 2:7

Respiratory Minibooks
Lesson 6

Paste your Respiratory
Minibooks onto this
page.

What Does the Bible say About Breath?

Look up the word "breath" in your concordance and study the use of the word in the Bible. What does God's Word say about breath? When was the word first used? Write about your findings and share them with your family.

How Many Breaths?

Compare how many breaths you take when you're resting to how many breaths you take after exercising. Count the number of times you inhale in one minute. Then, do jumping jacks for one minute. Stop and count how many breaths you take in one minute after exercising. Is there a difference? Can you explain why?

Molecule Movement

Write a story about a molecule of oxygen that moves from the air, into your mouth, down your trachea and into your lungs. Where does it go? What does it think? How does it feel about how it is being used? You might even begin with where it was made (possibly by a plant). Have fun with your story!

Blue Breath

The air you breathe in is filled with oxygen, but do you have oxygen in the air you breathe out? If so, how much oxygen comes out of your breath along with the carbon dioxide? Let's find out! When you exhale carbon dioxide, if it mixes with water, it will form a weak acid called carbonic acid. This acid turns into a substance called bromothymol blue. Let's do an activity to find out if you breathe out more carbon dioxide after exercising.

You will need:
A glass
A straw
Bromothymol blue (can be purchased from pet stores)
A timer

Fill the glass with water. Add four drops of bromothymol blue to the water. (The water should be light blue.) Place the straw in the water. Now take a deep breath, then exhale into the straw. (DO NOT DRINK THIS WATER!) What happened to the water?

Now, run in place for five minutes and repeat the same activity. What happens when you blow in the water after exercising? Why do you think this happens?

Book Suggestion

Lungs: Your Respiratory System by Seymor Simon. Acclaimed science writer Seymour Simon has teamed up with the Smithsonian Institution to explore the important journey that air takes in and out of your lungs.

My Respiratory Projects
Lesson 6

What I did:

What I did:

What I learned:

What I learned:

Fascinating Facts

about

BLOOD

LESSON 7

Fascinating Facts

about

BLOOD

LESSON 7

WHAT DO YOU REMEMBER?
LESSON 7

1. Why did Jesus give Himself as the sacrifice for our sins?

2. What does a person have to do to be forgiven for their sins once and for all and receive life everlasting?

3. What are the four functions of blood?

4. Name the four basic components of blood.

5. What should you do if you are bleeding seriously?

6. Where are your blood cells made?

7. Why is it important to give people the right type of blood?

8. What are the four blood types (not including the Rh factor)?

BLOOD

LESSON 7

Red Blood Cells   **White Blood Cells**   **Platelets**   **Plasma**

APOLOGIA of FAITH

VOCABULARY CROSSWORD
BLOOD

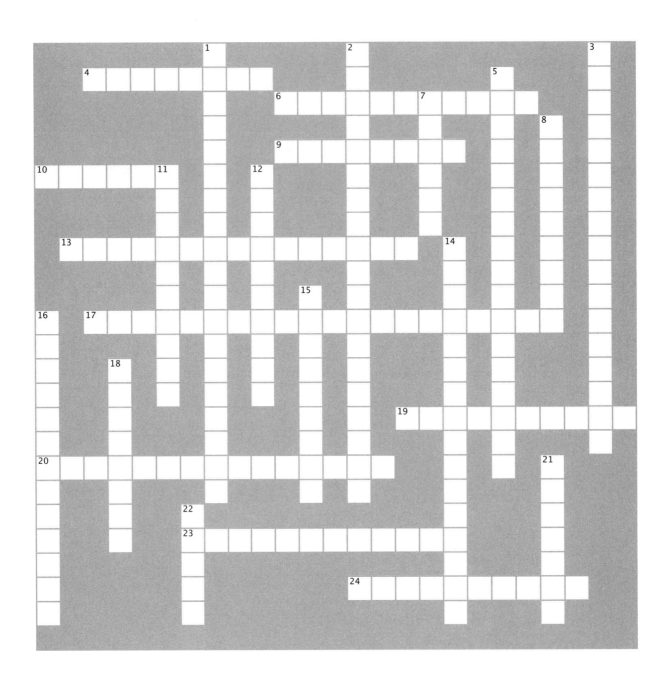

ARTERIES

VENULES

CAPILLARIES

PLASMA

RED BLOOD CELLS

HEMOGLOBIN

LEUKOCYTES

ANTIGENS

VEINS

ARTERIOLES

PLATELETS

HORMONES

ERYTHROCYTES

PHAGOCYTES

ANEMIA

STEM CELLS

CIRCULATORY SYSTEM

OXYGENATED BLOOD

WHITE BLOOD CELLS

DEOXYGENATED BLOOD

BLOOD CLOTTING PROCESS

BLOOD TRANSFUSION

UNIVERSAL DONOR BLOOD

UNIVERSAL RECIPIENTS

VOCABULARY CROSSWORD
BLOOD

Across

4. Chemical messengers that travel the body via the bloodstream in order to control and coordinate complex processes, such as growth and metabolism.
6. Blood vessels with very thin walls. They join the smallest artioles to the smallest venules.
9. Vessels that carry blood away from your heart.
10. The liquid part of your blood, made up of 90% water.
13. Lymphatic/immune system cells that travel throughout your body, attempting to destroy harmful bacteria and viruses. THREE WORDS
17. The sealing of cuts. This process keeps your blood from leaking out and helps to prevent the invasion of harmful bacteria. THREE WORDS
19. Special white blood cells that eat dangerous or worn-out cells.
20. Blood that is carrying oxygen to the cells. TWO WORDS
23. Another name for red blood cells.
24. Another name for white blood cells.

Down

1. People who can receive all blood types because they have both A and B antigens on their red blood cells. TWO WORDS
2. The blood type that has neither A nor B antigens and can be given to nearly any person. THREE WORDS
3. The system that carries your blood throughout your body. TWO WORDS
5. Blood that has given up some of its oxygen and picked up carbon dioxide. TWO WORDS
7. A condition that results from not having enough red blood cells.
8. Fragments of cells that are carried in your blood. They aid in the blood clotting process.
11. Vessels that branch out from the arteries becoming "little arteries."
12. The special oxygen carrying protein that red blood cells make and use.
14. The transferring of blood from one person to another. TWO WORDS
15. Cells that have the ability to become any kind of cell they need to be. TWO WORDS
16. These turn your blood red and make up 40% of the solids found in a drop of blood. THREE WORDS
18. These special markers are attached to your cells. The ones attached to red blood cells determine the type of blood you have.
21. "Little veins" that come together to form larger veins.
22. Vessels that return blood to your heart.

Copywork

But if we walk in the light, as he is in the light, we have fellowship with one another, and the blood of Jesus, his Son, purifies us from all sin.

1 John 1:7

_____

_____

_____

_____

_____

_____

_____

Copywork

But if we walk in the light, as he is in the light, we have fellowship with one another, and the blood of Jesus, his Son, purifies us from all sin.

1 John 1:7

Blood Minibooks

Lesson 7

Paste your Blood Shutter
Books onto this page.

Study the Eternal Significance of Blood

Find out what the Bible says about the blood of Jesus. Look up the word "blood" in a concordance. Read the verses that talk about Jesus' blood. What is its significance? What did the blood of Jesus accomplish? Write about your findings and share them with someone who has never considered the eternal significance of Jesus' shed blood.

Research Blood

Use the Internet or your library to research different aspects of blood. Some interesting topics to research include: different diseases that are spread through the blood, various blood disorders or diseases (such as hemophilia or leukemia), and different white blood cell counts and what they mean. Organize your research into a report and present it to your family or homeschool group.

DVD Suggestions

Red River of Life: Moody Science Classics Series. In this Christian DVD you'll learn about blood and how it carries oxygen to every part of your body. You'll also learn how the shed blood of Jesus Christ is the source of eternal life. (Elementary and up- 30 minutes)

Standard Deviants School - Anatomy, Program 5 - The Circulatory System (Classroom Edition). This fast paced, action packed DVD takes you on an exciting journey into the circulatory system.

My Blood Project
Lesson 7

What I did:

What I learned:

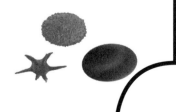

Fascinating Facts

about the

CARDIOVASCULAR SYSTEM

LESSON 8

Fascinating Facts

about the

CARDIOVASCULAR SYSTEM
LESSON 8

How Blood Flows Through The Heart

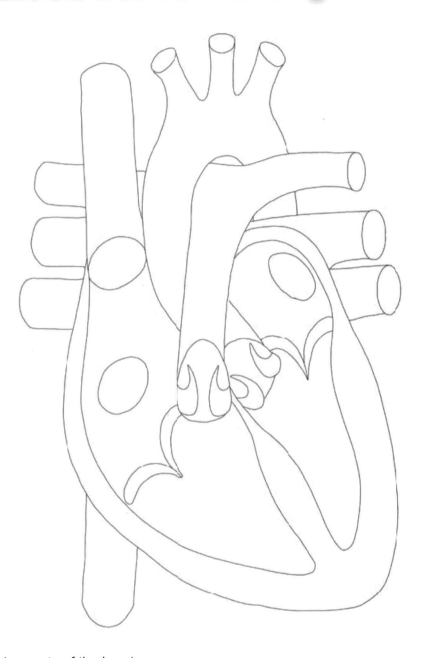

Label the following parts of the heart:

Right Ventricle   Aorta
Right Atrium   Pulmonary Vein
Left Ventricle   Pulmonary Artery
Left Atrium   Superior Vena Cave
Inferior Vena Cava

Color the chambers and vessels that contain deoxygenated blood blue.

Color the chambers and vessels that contain oxygenated blood red.

Use arrows to indicate the path that blood takes as it travels into the heart, out the pulmonary arteries, back into the heart from the pulmonary veins, and out from the aorta.

NAME _____   DATE _____

WHAT DO YOU REMEMBER?
LESSON 8

1. What do we call the top two chambers of your heart?

2. What do we call the bottom two chambers?

3. What are the veins leading from the lungs into the heart called?

4. What is the artery leading from the heart to the lungs called?

5. What is the main artery that takes blood out of the heart to the body?

6. What are the names of the two veins that bring deoxygenated blood from the tissues of the body back to the heart?

7. What is it that you are hearing when you hear your heart beat?

8. What do the two numbers in a person's blood pressure mean?

Copywork

That if you confess with your mouth, "Jesus is Lord," and believe in your heart that God raised him from the dead, you will be saved.

Romans 10:9

Copywork

That if you confess with your mouth, "Jesus is Lord," and believe in your heart that God raised him from the dead, you will be saved.

Romans 10:9

VOCABULARY CROSSWORD CARDIOVASCULAR SYSTEM

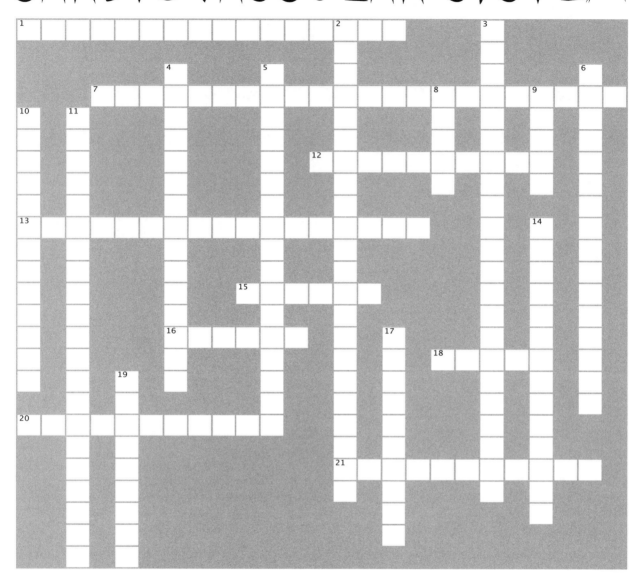

PULMONARY VEINS
ATRIA
PLAQUE
INFERIOR VENA CAVA
MYOCARDIUM
INTERATRIAL SEPTUM
ENDOCARDIUM
SEMILUNAR VALVES
PACEMAKER
BLOOD PRESSURE
PULSE

VENTRICLES
VALVES
AORTA
PULMONARY ARTERIES
SUPERIOR VENA CAVA
PERICARDIUM
INTERVENTRICULAR SEPTUM
ATRIOVENTRICULAR VALVES
SYSTOLIC BLOOD PRESSURE
DIASTOLIC BLOOD PRESSURE

VOCABULARY CROSSWORD
CARDIOVASCULAR SYSTEM

Across

1. The large vein that collects blood from the lower parts of the body. THREE WORDS
7. The thick, muscular wall between the two ventricles. TWO WORDS
12. The two lower chambers of the heart. These muscular chambers push the blood out of your heart.
13. The only arteries that carry deoxygenated blood. They carry blood from the right ventricle to the lungs. TWO WORDS
15. Deposits of fatty material that build up inside the blood vessels.
16. "Doors" that open and close and are located between each atrium and ventricle and between each ventricle and the blood vessel leaving that ventricle.
18. The largest artery in the body. It carries oxygenated blood away from the heart to arteries serving the body.
20. A special fibrous sac that holds the heart in place.
21. The thin, smooth tissue that lines the inside walls of the heart.

Down

2. Two of the four valves found in the heart. These valves are placed between the atrium and ventricle on each side. TWO WORDS
3. The second number in a person's blood pressure. It indicates the pressure against the arterial walls when the ventricles relax. THREE WORDS
4. Two of the four valves found in the heart. These half-moon shaped valves keep the blood from flowing backwards into the ventricles from the aorta and pulmonary artery when the heart relaxes between beats. TWO WORDS
5. The thin wall between the two atria. TWO WORDS
6. The large vein that collects blood from the upper parts of the body. THREE WORDS
8. The top two chambers of the heart.
9. The momentary stretching of arteries caused by the rush of blood forced out of the heart with each beat (contraction).
10. A measurement of the force of the blood pushing against the walls of the arteries. TWO WORDS
11. The first number in a person's blood pressure. It indicates the pressure against the arterial walls when the ventricles contract. THREE WORDS
14. Veins that carry oxygenated blood from the lungs to the heart. TWO WORDS
17. The heart muscle. It's the thickest layer of the heart.
19. A unique cluster of cells inside the heart that causes the heart to beat on its own.

Cardiovascular Minibooks
LESSON 8

Paste your Cardio Tuck
In Envelopes onto this
page.

What Does the Bible say About the Heart?

God's word has a lot to say about the heart. Use a concordance to find all the references to the heart in the Bible. Read all the verses over the next week. Which verses speak to you most? Write about them in your journal or copy them onto index cards and memorize them. Be sure to share at least one of the verses with a friend or family member.

Find Your Resting Heart Rate

The resting heart rate of a healthy adult is between 60-100 beats per minute. Youths are known to have resting heart rates well over 100 beats per minute. People who exercise consistently have lower heart rates than those who don't exercise. Why do you think that is?

Make a Model of the Human Heart with Clay

Although this may be a bit difficult to get just right, use different colored clay to make an exterior model of the human heart. Be sure to include the veins and arteries leading in and out of the heart.

Heart Dissection

If you're really brave you can watch a heart being disassembled! Do an Internet search for: heart dissection. You will find links to videos of different types of heart dissections. How would you like to dissect a heart yourself! Check your homeschool group to see if they are offering a dissection lab for an animal's heart.

Write Your Own Zoe Story

You read the story of Zoe in this lesson. Now it's your turn to write your own story about a blood cell's journey through the body. Give your blood cell a name and a personality. Read back through the lesson to remember what you learned before you begin writing. Be creative and have fun describing the journey of a blood cell!

Book Suggestions

The Heart: Our Circulatory System by Seymour Simon. Acclaimed science writer Seymour Simon has teamed up with the Smithsonian Institution to explore the heart, blood and other parts of the body's circulatory system.

The Magic School Bus Has a Heart: Scholastic Reader Level 2 by Anne Capeci. Mrs. Frizzle's class travels through the bloodstream and learns about the heart's job and how it works with the lungs. Hop on the Magic School Bus and find out what's at the heart of it all!

My Cardio Projects
Lesson 8

What I did:

What I did:

What I learned:

What I learned:

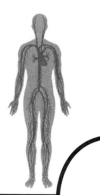

Fascinating Facts

about the

NERVOUS AND ENDOCRINE SYSTEMS

LESSON 9

Fascinating Facts

about the

NERVOUS AND ENDOCRINE SYSTEMS

LESSON 9

WHAT DO YOU REMEMBER?
LESSON 9

1. Name the three parts of the brain we discussed.

2. What part of a neuron receives information?

3. What part sends the information on its way?

4. Where do you find the nucleus in a neuron?

5. What does a sensory neuron do?

6. What does a motor neuron do?

7. What is the somatic nervous system?

8. What is the autonomic nervous system?

9. What does the endocrine system do?

BRAIN

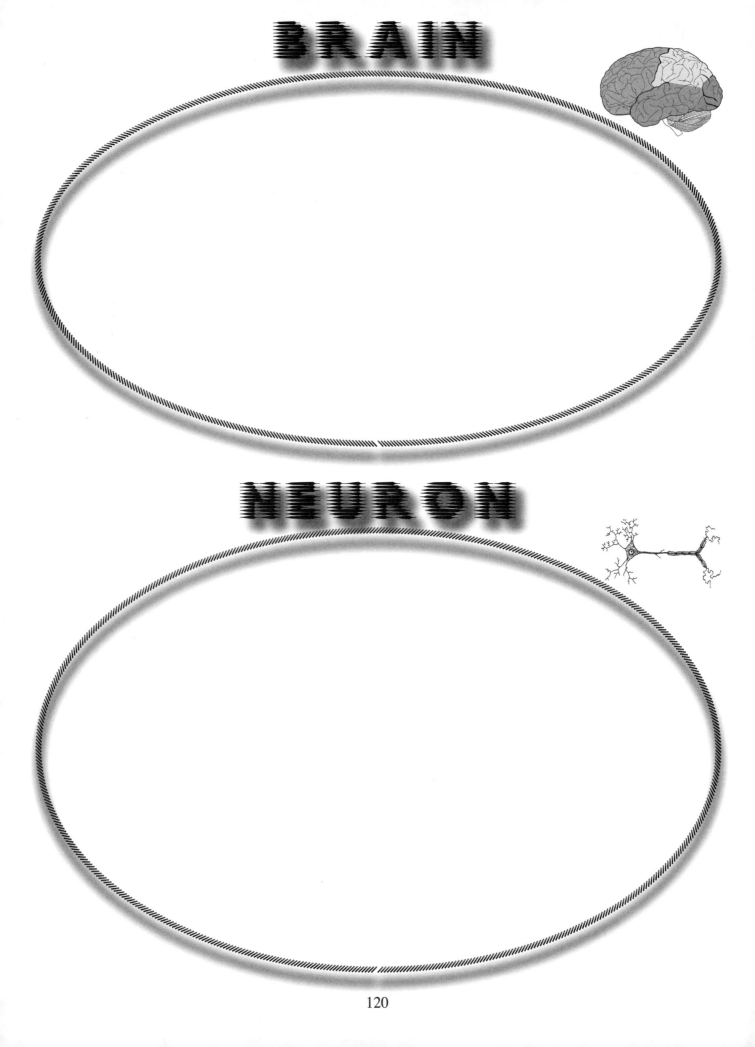

NEURON

VENN DIAGRAM
LESSON 9

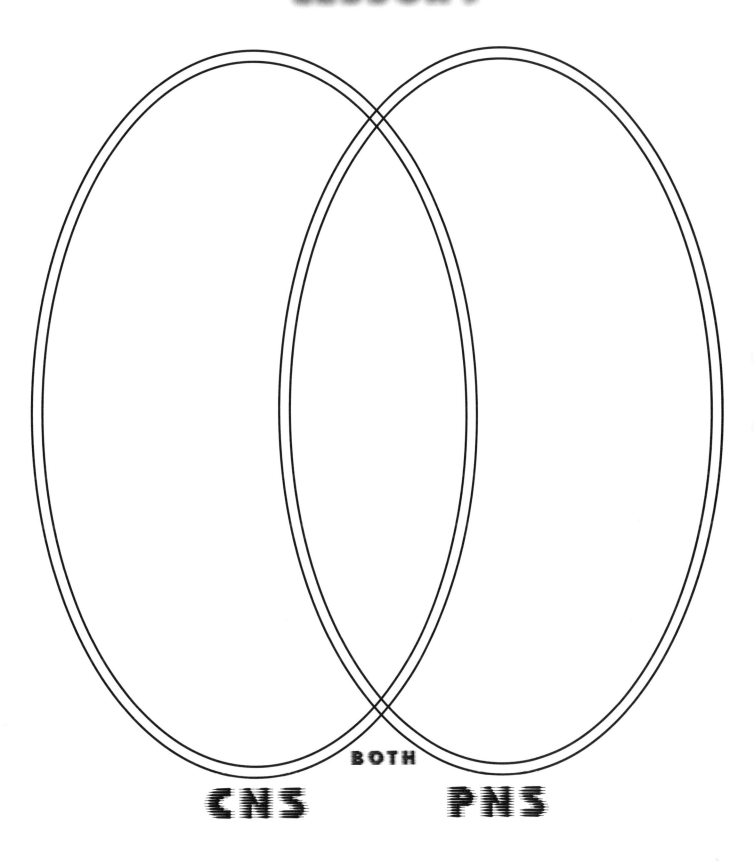

BOTH

CNS

PNS

Copywork

You will keep in perfect peace him
whose mind is steadfast, because
he trusts in you.

Isaiah 26:3

Copywork

You will keep in perfect peace him whose mind is steadfast, because he trusts in you.

Isaiah 26:3

VOCABULARY CROSSWORD
NERVOUS SYSTEM

PERIPHERAL NERVOUS SYSTEM
AUTONOMIC NERVOUS SYSTEM
CEREBRAL CORTEX
CENTRAL NERVOUS SYSTEM
NEUROTRANSMITTERS
MOTOR NEURONS
SOMATIC NERVOUS SYSTEM

INTERNEURON
NERVOUS SYSTEM
BRAINSTEM
NEURONS
MYELIN SHEATH
SYNAPSE
SENSORY NEURONS

CELL BODY
INTEGRATION
AXON
NERVES
CEREBRUM
DENDRITE
CEREBELLUM

VOCABULARY CROSSWORD NERVOUS SYSTEM

Across

1. The part of a neuron that contains the nucleus and receives information from the dendrites. TWO WORDS
3. A function of the brain that sorts and processes information, making it understandable and usable.
7. Neurons that send information to your spinal cord and brain for processing. TWO WORDS
9. The largest part of the brain where most of your conscious actions are controlled, and thoughts are thought.
10. The "little brain" that controls your complex muscle movements, helping you to maintain balance.
11. The most important cells in the nervous system. They receive, store, and process information, as well as send messages throughout the body.
15. Contains nerves that spread out from the central nervous system to the outer edges of the body. THREE WORDS
17. The very tiny space between the axon terminal of one neuron and the dendrite of another.
19. A type of neuron that is found between (and connects) other neurons.
21. Chemicals at the end of an axon that transmit information from one neuron to another.

Down

2. Connects the brain to the spinal cord and controls things like your breathing and heartbeat.
4. The part of the peripheral nervous system that works automatically. It controls your smooth muscles so your organs can function without you thinking about them. THREE WORDS
5. Contains the brain and spinal cord. THREE WORDS
6. The part of the peripheral nervous system that is responsible for the voluntary movements you make. THREE WORDS
8. The two-part (central and peripheral) system that controls a huge number of activities in your body. TWO WORDS
12. Neurons that send information from your brain and spinal cord to your body, telling your muscles and other organs what to do. TWO WORDS
13. The fatty tissue wrapped around an axon that allows information to travel more quickly down the axon. TWO WORDS
14. The folded outer part of your cerebrum. TWO WORDS
16. The part of a neuron that transmits information from the nucleus to different parts of the body.
18. Bundles of neuron axons running together. They gather information from inside and outside your body and send it to your brain. They also carry commands from your brain to your body.
20. One of the "arms" of a neuron that reaches out in many directions and gathers information.

VOCABULARY CROSSWORD
ENDOCRINE SYSTEM

ENDOCRINE SYSTEM   HOMEOSTASIS   THYROID GLAND   PITUITARY GLAND
ADRENAL GLANDS   HORMONES   THYMUS GLAND

Across

5. The glands that release the hormone epinephrine (the hormone released during the fight or flight response). TWO WORDS
6. The gland located on the front of the neck that produces a hormone that speeds up the rate at which almost all cells burn their fuel for energy. TWO WORDS
7. Chemicals produced in your glands that travel the blood stream to interact with specific cells or organs, telling them to perform precise functions.

Down

1. The gland in your brain that is the central controller for many other hormone releasing glands. TWO WORDS
2. The system that operates through hormones to coordinate and control many of the activities that go on in your body. TWO WORDS
3. The condition that occurs when all the systems of your body are working together to maintain a stable, healthy condition.
4. The gland that helps the body's defense system by producing the hormones responsible for the development of a certain type of white blood cell. TWO WORDS

Test Your Auditory Memory

Here is an activity you can do with a friend to improve your brain function. Call out a series of six numbers. Can your friend recite the numbers exactly as you called them out? Now see if you can recite the six numbers your friend calls out. Most people can do six numbers. Not everyone can remember seven. Very, very few people can recite nine numbers that are called out. With practice, you might be able to build up to nine!

Test Your Visual Memory

Cut out 1 inch x 1 inch squares of different colored construction paper. You will need 15 squares of each color: red, blue, yellow, white and black.

Sit across from your friend and put a folder on the table between you. Place the folder in an open upright position (like a tent) so that your friend cannot see you place the colored squares. Put six colored squares in any order. Then, carefully remove the folder. Give your friend three seconds to look at the squares. Now cover them up with a black piece of construction paper. Next, have your friend rebuild the squares in the order in which you put them. Of course, your friend's squares will be opposite your order because your friend was seeing them backwards. Once your friend is done, lift up the black piece of paper and compare. If your friend was successful, let her give you a chance to do it. This time try with seven squares. Then try with eight. To make things even more challenging, place the squares in a unique pattern or shape. Also, you can reduce the time allowed for looking at the pattern. Or, if a three second look is too challenging, you can increase the amount of time for looking and slowly decrease it as you build your skills.

Build Your Brain

Research has shown that challenging the mind with games and activities that require a great deal of mental processing can actually keep people from aging mentally. It can also improve a person's overall cognitive or thinking ability. It's just like physical exercise. If you exercise your brain, it will grow stronger. Additionally, studies suggest that if you do not exercise your brain, you will lose valuable brain functioning, perhaps permanently. Yet, we can actually grow neural pathways at any age. So, although you need to use it or lose it, if you work hard, you can grow your brain! That's another reason to learn as much as you can and try to remember what you learned. Why not begin learning some of the games and participating in some of the activities that have shown to develop neural pathways? Here are some suggestions:

Learn to play Chess

Learn to play Bridge

Learn to play Sudoku

Listen to Classical Music

Learn to play an instrument

Learn a foreign language

Learn a new sport

127

My Nervous System Projects
Lesson 9

What I did:

What I did:

What I learned:

What I learned:

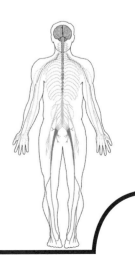

NERVOUS SYSTEM MINIBOOK
LESSON 9

Paste your Nervous
System Layered Book
onto this page.

Fascinating Facts

about the

NERVOUS SYSTEM

LESSON 10

WHAT DO YOU REMEMBER?
LESSON 10

1. Name the four lobes in the cerebrum.

2. Which lobe is responsible for speech and language?

3. Which lobe is responsible for your emotions?

4. Which lobe processes smell and memory as well as tone and loudness?

5. Which lobe processes sensory information and integrates it to determine where you are in relation to your surroundings?

6. Which lobe processes visual information?

7. Which side of your brain is more active when you are doing math?

8. Which is more active when you are working on a piece of art?

9. How does myelin help your neurons?

10. Which part of the brain is responsible for keeping you balanced?

11. What is the reflex arc?

12. Why are interneurons and interconnections between neurons important?

NERVOUS SYSTEM

LESSON 10

Brain Lobes

_____
_____
_____
_____
_____
_____
_____
_____
_____
_____
_____

Brain Hemispheres

_____
_____
_____
_____
_____
_____
_____
_____

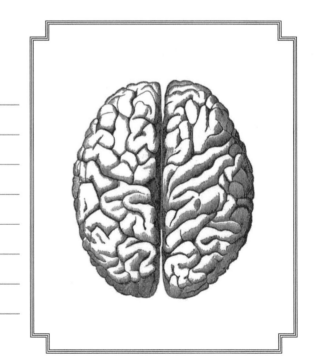

Myelin

_____
_____
_____
_____

Cerebellum and Brain Stem

_____
_____
_____
_____
_____

Spinal Cord and Reflex Arc

_____
_____
_____
_____
_____
_____
_____

CEREBRAL LOBES

LESSON 10

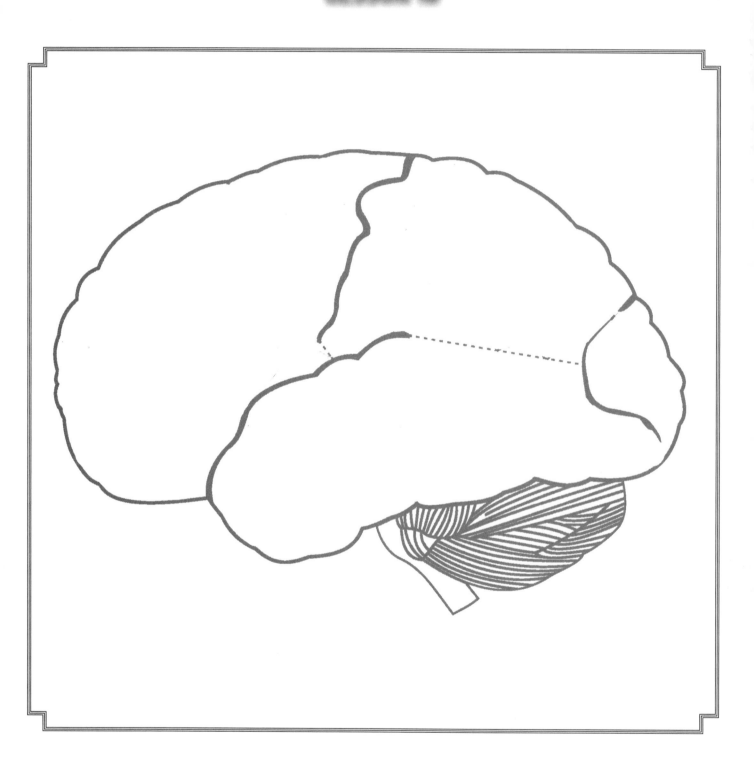

Frontal Lobe   **Temporal Lobe**   **Occipital Lobe**   **Parietal Lobe**

VOCABULARY CROSSWORD
NERVOUS SYSTEM EXTENDED

GRAY MATTER   REFLEX ARC   WHITE MATTER   CEREBROSPINAL FLUID
FRONTAL LOBE   PARIETAL LOBE   OCCIPITAL LOBE   RIGHT HEMISPHERE
TEMPORAL LOBE   LEFT HEMISPHERE

Across

6. A special fluid between the skull and brain that helps cushion the brain and keep it comfortably in place. TWO WORDS
7. The right half of the cerebrum. TWO WORDS
8. One of the four lobes of the cerebrum. It is located behind the frontal lobe and processes all sorts of sensory information. TWO WORDS
9. The lobe of the cerebrum that is located near your temple. It processes both smells and memory. TWO WORDS
10. When an interneuron in the spinal cord decides to activate a motor neuron without waiting for the brain to give instructions. TWO WORDS

Down

1. The outer surface of the brain is called _____. Neuron cell bodies give it its color. TWO WORDS
2. The lobe located in the back part of the cerebrum. It processes visual information. TWO WORDS
3. The left half of the cerebrum. TWO WORDS
4. The lobe located in the front part of the cerebrum. It is where speech and language are learned and used, purposeful movements initiated, and problems solved. TWO WORDS
5. The inner surface of the brain is called _____. Myelin gives it its color. TWO WORDS

Copywork

For to be carnally minded is
death; but to be spiritually minded
is life and peace.

Romans 8:6

Copywork

For to be carnally minded is death;
but to be spiritually minded is life
and peace.

Romans 8:6

BRAIN MINIBOOK
LESSON 10

Paste your Brain Book
onto this page.

Creative Writing Assignment

Write a newspaper article describing what your brain did today. You can read the sports page for ideas on how to describe the play by play actions. Tell your readers which players (parts of the brain) did what during the day.

Foot Dominance

You probably know whether you are right- or left-handed, but are you right- or left-footed? Are you right- or left-eyed? Are you right- or left-eared? All these things are dominated by a particular side of your brain. Let's find out which you are.

To find out if you are right- or left-footed, find an open space and try to do a cartwheel. With which foot did you begin? If it's the opposite of your handedness, then see which foot you prefer when kicking a ball. You can be ambidextrous, or have both feet dominant at different times.

Eye Dominance

Do you know which eye takes command when you are seeing? Look at something far away. Then, line up one of your fingers with that object to block it out. Now, keeping your finger there, close one eye, then the other. When you close your weaker eye, the object will remain blocked. However, when you open and close your "seeing" or dominant eye, your finger will jump back and forth.

Here's another way to find out. Cut a 1 inch circle out of the middle of a piece of notebook paper. Now, using both eyes, look through the hole in the paper at a distant object. Now, bring the paper closer and closer to your face, keeping the distant object in focus. To which eye did you bring the paper? That's your dominant eye!

Ear Dominance

You also have a dominant ear. Let's see which one hears the best. If your friend says she needs to tell you a secret as she comes toward you, which ear do you give her?

Now, imagine you want to listen to a conversation in another room through the wall. Which ear do you put up to the wall? That's your dominant ear!

Book Suggestion

Understanding Your Brain by Usborne Books. Using lively text, colorful diagrams and comical illustrations, this book "lifts the lid" on what's inside children's heads.

My Nervous System Projects
Lesson 10

What I did:

What I did:

What I learned:

What I learned:

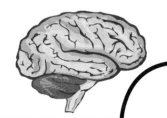

Fascinating Facts

about your

SENSES
LESSON 11

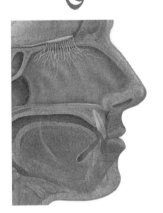

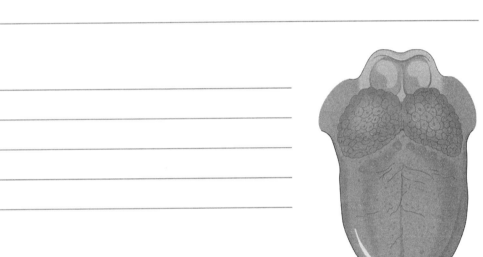

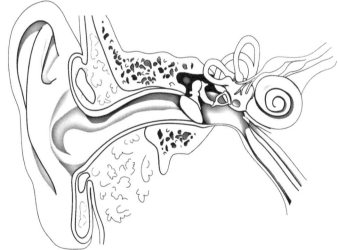

WHAT DO YOU REMEMBER?
LESSON 11

1. What is the part of your nose that holds your olfactory cells called?

2. How are odors received and transferred to the brain?

3. Where are your taste buds found?

4. What are the five taste sensations?

5. What is the pinna?

6. Why do ears make wax?

7. Name the three bones in the middle ear.

8. What are otoliths?

9. What is the sclera?

10. What is the pupil?

11. What is the iris of an eye?

12. What is the fovea?

13. What cells enable you to see in color?

14. What cells enable you to see in dim light?

15. Name some of the ways God added special protection for your eyes.

Diagram of Eye
LESSON 11

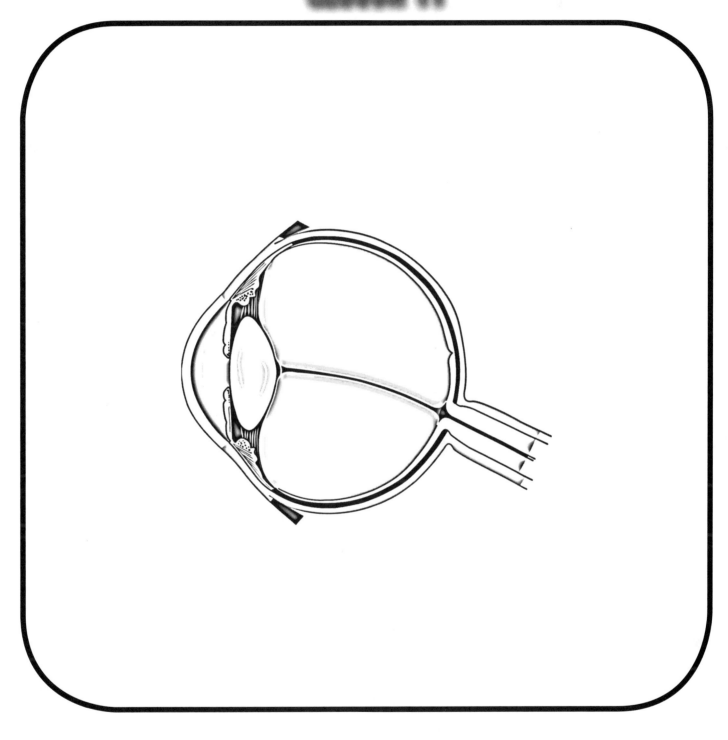

Retina	**Fovea**	**Cornea**
Ciliary Muscle	**Optic Nerve**	**Pupil**
Aqueous Humor	**Sclera**	**Lens**

VOCABULARY CROSSWORD
MOUTH, NOSE AND EARS

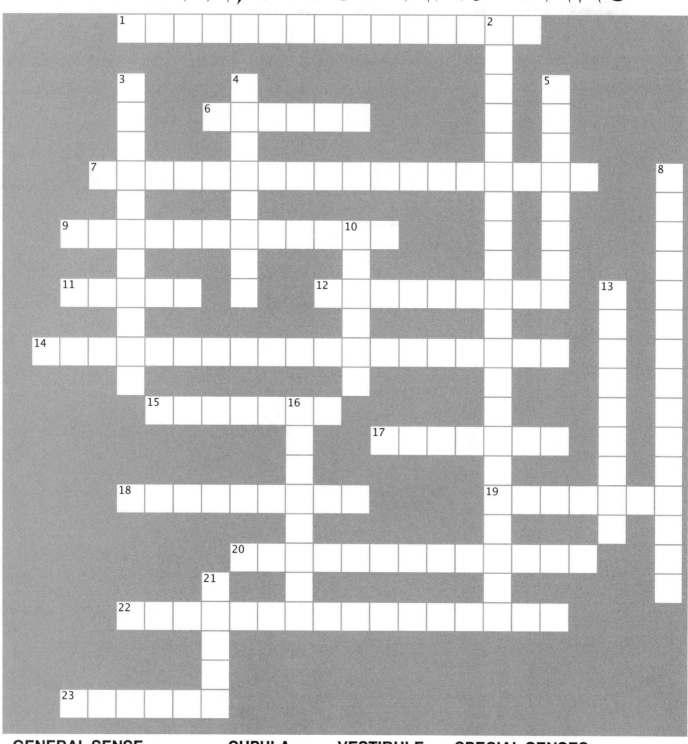

GENERAL SENSE
OLFACTORY GLANDS
EXTERNAL EAR
AUDITORY OSSICLES
OLFACTORY EPITHELIUM
SEMICIRCULAR CANALS

CUPULA
OTOLITHS
MACULA
STATIC
COCHLEA
DYNAMIC

VESTIBULE
CILIA
PAPILLAE
PINNA
INNER EAR
EARDRUM

SPECIAL SENSES
TASTE BUDS
MIDDLE EAR
OLFACTORY SYSTEM
EXTERNAL AUDITORY CANAL

VOCABULARY CROSSWORD MOUTH, NOSE AND EARS

Across

1. The system that gives you your sense of smell. TWO WORDS
6. A small spot inside your inner ear that contains a thick, gel-like fluid and houses teeny-tiny stones (otoliths).
7. The three structures inside the inner ear that contain fluid and help to control your balance. TWO WORDS
9. Another name for your sense of touch. It is the one sense that your whole body can experience. TWO WORDS
11. Tiny hairs projecting from each olfactory cell. They greatly increase the surface area so that even very faint odors can be detected.
12. The five taste sensations (sweet, sour, salty, bitter, umami) are detected by these special receptors. TWO WORDS
14. A cluster of olfactory cells, located in the roof of the upper nose, that senses the chemicals that produce smells. TWO WORDS
15. The sense of balance that informs you about active movements of your head.
17. The thin membrane that vibrates in response to sound waves and transmits the vibrations to the auditory ossicles.
18. The middle part of the ear, containing the malleus, incus and stapes. TWO WORDS
19. The snail shell shaped structure inside the inner ear that converts sound waves to nerve signals.
20. The five senses that occur as a result of specific organs at special places in your body. TWO WORDS
22. The three tiny bones inside your middle ear: the malleus, incus and stapes. TWO WORDS
23. A tiny sail-like structure inside the inner ear that helps to keep you balanced.

Down

2. The part of your ear leading from the pinna to the ear drum. THREE WORDS
3. The outer part of the ear, containing the pinna, external auditory canal and eardrum. TWO WORDS
4. The visible "bumps" on your tongue. Some of them house your taste buds.
5. Tiny stones inside your ears that help detect the movement of your head.
8. Glands that produce the mucus layer in which the cilia float. TWO WORDS
10. The sense of balance that tells you the position of your head and helps you to maintain your posture when you are not actively moving.
13. The part of the inner ear where your static sense of balance is located.
16. The inner part of the ear, containing the semicircular canals and the cochlea. TWO WORDS
21. The part of the ear you see from the outside, also called the auricle.

VOCABULARY CROSSWORD
EYES

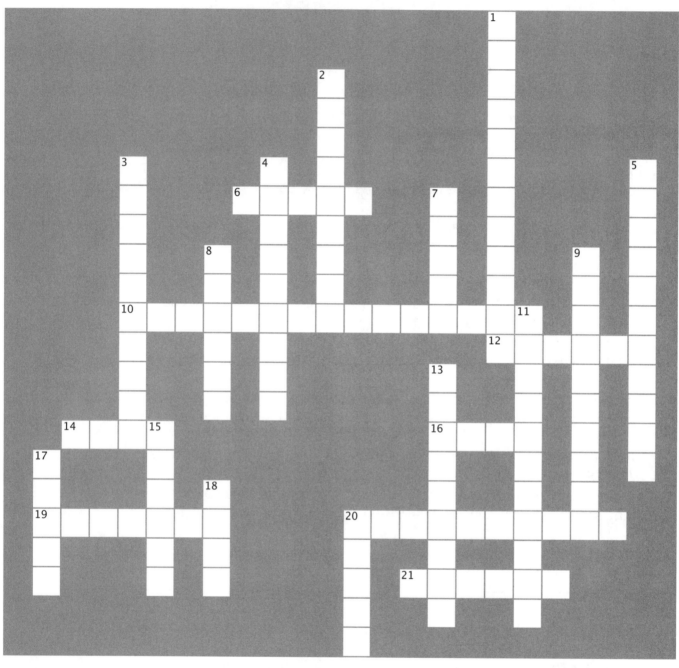

SCLERA
IRIS
AQUEOUS HUMOR
RETINA
CONES
FOVEA
ASTIGMATISM
MYOPIA

HYPEROPIA
BLIND SPOT
BINOCULAR VISION
TEARS
TEAR DUCTS
PINKEYE
FARSIGHTED

CORNEA
PUPIL
LENS
RODS
OPTIC NERVE
COLORBLIND
NEARSIGHTED

VOCABULARY CROSSWORD
EYES

Across

6. A wet substance designed to moisten, cleanse and disinfect your eyes.
10. God's design for the eyes of people and some animals. It enables the eyes to work together in order to locate objects more accurately. TWO WORDS
12. The lining of the inside of the back of your eye. It contains the rods and the cones.
14. Special cells spread all over your retina that allow you to see in dim light.
16. The colored circle behind the cornea. It automatically adjusts the size of the pupil, controlling the amount of light entering the eye.
19. A condition that results when the conjunctiva (protective covering over the white part of the eye) becomes infected and turns pink.
20. A person that can see things well far away but cannot see things very well up close is said to be _____.
21. The clear "window" in the front of your eye through which light passes.

Down

1. A clear, watery fluid that flows through the pupil and moistens the back of the cornea, the iris, and the lens of the eye. TWO WORDS
2. A farsighted person is said to have _____.
3. A person who cannot see all the colors they should is said to be _____.
4. Special tubes that lead from the corners of your eyes into your nose. TWO WORDS
5. A visual defect resulting from the cornea being shaped incorrectly. As a result, everything is a bit blurry.
7. Special cells concentrated in one spot on your retina that allow you to see in color.
8. A nearsighted person is said to have _____.
9. The nerve that sends information from the retinal cells to the brain. TWO WORDS
11. A person that can see things well up close but cannot see things very well far away is said to be _____.
13. The spot in your eye where there are no rods or cones. It is the place where the optic nerve is located. TWO WORDS
15. The white outer layer of your eyeball. It covers all but the cornea.
17. The round black spot in the middle of your iris. Light enters this part of your eye.
18. The part of your eye that enables you to see near and far. It focuses light rays, very much like the lens of a camera.
20. The area of the retina where the cones are concentrated. It is where your vision is most sharply focused.

I will instruct you and teach you in the way which you should go; I will counsel you with My eye upon you."

Psalm 32:8

Copywork

I will instruct you and teach you in the way which you should go; I will counsel you with My eye upon you."

Psalm 32:8

SENSES MINIBOOK
LESSON 11

Paste your Five Senses
Tab Book onto this page.

What Does the Bible say About the Eyes?

The Bible talks about the eyes quite a bit. Use a concordance to find and read all the verses that talk about the eyes. Write down what you learn about eyes as you read. How can your eyes aid in or hinder your spiritual life?

Make an Ear Drum Model

Make a model of your ear drum with an empty bathroom tissue tube, a balloon big enough to fit over it, and a rubber band. Cut the thin portion off the balloon and stretch it over one end of the tube. Secure it with a rubber band. Now, put your finger on the balloon and speak through the other end of the tube. Can you feel the balloon vibrate? This is how your eardrum works.

You can extend this activity by making an entire model of the ear. You might use clay to form the inner ear organs, and craft supplies to make the bones.

Follow Your Nose

Let's see if you can locate where a smell comes from without the use of your eyes. Place strong aromas, such as perfume and vanilla, on cotton balls. Now, have a friend hide the cotton around a large room. With a blindfold on, see how long it takes you to locate the cotton balls. Have your friend give it a try as well. Who has a better sense of smell?

Turn Off That Sound

You may not realize it, but your house is full of sounds that you have become accustomed to. Try turning off and unplugging every single electric item for one whole day. Be sure to get your parents' permission to do this. You will want to plug your refrigerator back in right away so that your food does not spoil. However, I believe you'll be amazed at how really quiet it is.

Field Trip to an Optometrist

Schedule a field trip to visit an optometrist in order to learn about what they do to evaluate people's vision and how they find the right glasses for people. You might even have your eyes checked while you are there!

Balance Activity

How good is your balance? How long can you stand on one leg? How long can you stand on one leg with your eyes closed? Do you see how your eyes work with your ears to keep you balanced?

Here's another activity to test your balance. Find a thin board that is about two feet long and a foot wide. Now get a full can of food from the kitchen cabinet. Place the board on top of the can and carefully, with the help of an adult, step on either side of the board trying to balance it on the can.

My Senses Projects
Lesson 11

What I did:

What I did:

What I learned:

What I learned:

Fascinating Facts

about the

INTEGUMENTARY SYSTEM

LESSON 12

Fascinating Facts

about the

INTEGUMENTARY SYSTEM

LESSON 12

WHAT DO YOU REMEMBER?
LESSON 12

1. What is the system called that includes your skin, nails, and hair?

2. How do skin, nails, and hair grow?

3. What are the two layers of the skin?

4. What is the layer of tissue underneath those two layers?

5. What two important pigments are mostly responsible for skin color?

6. What do sebaceous glands make?

7. What does sweat do?

8. What are the three layers of a hair?

9. Which layer is sometimes missing?

10. Which layer of skin is responsible for making your fingerprints?

11. In both hair and nails, what is the name of the region in which new cells are made?

Diagram of Skin
Lesson 12

Epidermis	Hypodermis
Hair Follicle	Sweat Duct
Sweat Pore	Matrix
Dermis	Hair Shaft
Arrector Pili	Sebaceous Gland

FINGERPRINTS
LESSON 12

LEFT PINKY	LEFT RING	LEFT MIDDLE	LEFT INDEX	LEFT THUMB

RIGHT THUMB	RIGHT INDEX	RIGHT MIDDLE	RIGHT RING	RIGHT PINKY

What I did:

What I did:

What I learned:

What I learned:

BRAILLE ALPHABET CHALLENGE
LESSON 12

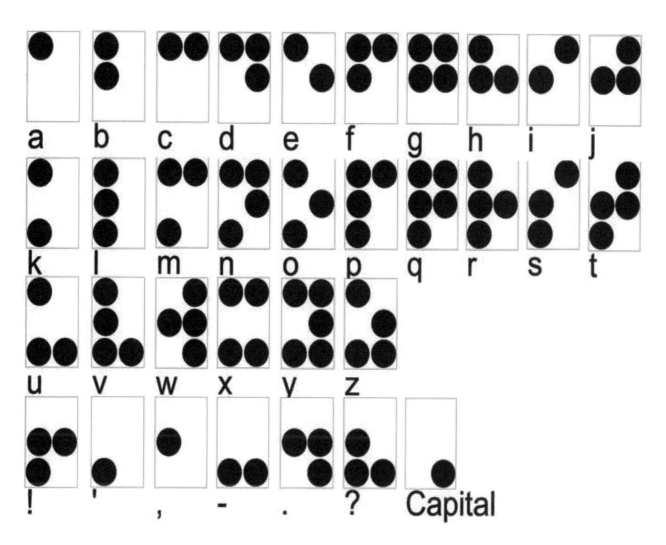

a b c d e f g h i j

k l m n o p q r s t

u v w x y z

! ' , - . ? Capital

Numbers

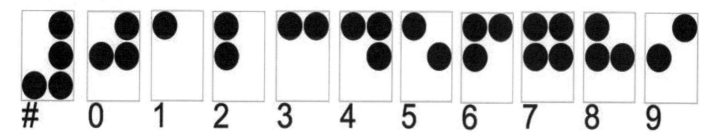

0 1 2 3 4 5 6 7 8 9

What I did:

What I did:

What I learned:

What I learned:

Copywork

Flesh gives birth to flesh, but
the Spirit gives birth to spirit.

John 3:6

Copywork

Flesh gives birth to flesh, but the
Spirit gives birth to spirit.

John 3:6

VOCABULARY CROSSWORD INTEGUMENTARY SYSTEM

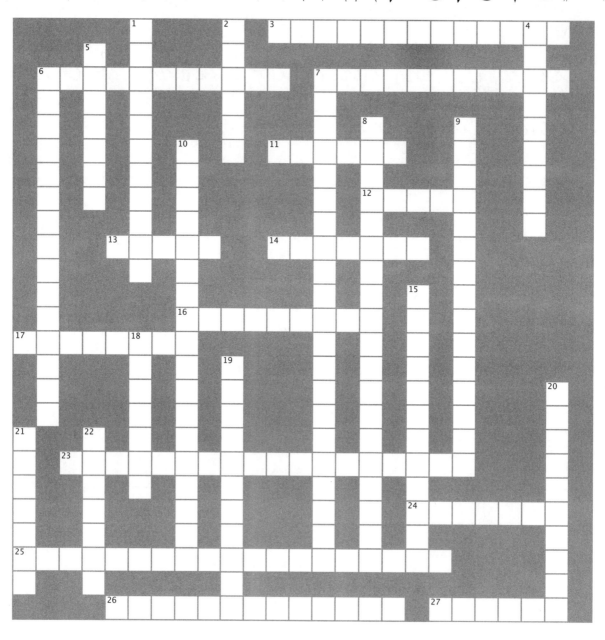

INTEGUMENTARY SYSTEM
DERMIS
MELANIN
ULTRAVIOLET
SEBUM
HARD KERATIN
MEDULLA
MEISSNER'S CORPUSCLES
PACINIAN CORPUSCLES
LUNULA

EPIDERMIS
HYPODERMIS
EPITHELIAL CELLS
CAROTENE
ELASTIN
SWEAT GLANDS
CUTICLE
CLEAVAGE LINES
HAIR FOLLICLE
NAIL BED

ADIPOSE TISSUE
KERATIN
MELANOCYTES
SEBACEOUS GLANDS
SHAFT
CORTEX
SUBCUTANEOUS TISSUE
NAIL FOLDS
HAIR FOLLICLE RECEPTORS

VOCABULARY CROSSWORD INTEGUMENTARY SYSTEM

Across

3. Patterns of tension in your skin. TWO WORDS
6. Glands in the dermis that produce sweat. TWO WORDS
7. The keratin made within the outer layers of hair cells, and within nail cells. TWO WORDS
11. The layer in which the color of your hair is found.
12. The part of the hair made up of dead, keratinized cells.
13. An oily substance which coats the skin and hair, keeping them smooth and supple.
14. Lots of this pigment will make a person's skin brown, olive or black.
16. Folds of skin that hold your nails in place. TWO WORDS
17. The pigment that gives the skin a slightly yellow tone.
23. Sensors in the dermis that can feel vibration and pressure. TWO WORDS
24. The outermost layer of a hair, made up of overlapping cells, like the shingles of a roof. This layer is clear.
25. Your skin (along with your nails, hair, sweat glands, and oil glands) makes up this complex group of tissues. TWO WORDS
26. Fat tissue. TWO WORDS
27. The innermost layer of your skin.

Down

1. Very high-energy light produced by the sun that can cause skin cancer.
2. The half moon shaped area of paleness beyond the cuticle of your nail. It is part of the nail matrix.
4. The outermost layer of your skin.
5. The innermost layer of your hair, made of loosely connected cells.
6. Oil glands that are like built-in skin lotion dispensers. TWO WORDS
7. Sensory neurons that are wrapped around each hair follicle. THREE WORDS
8. Tiny "ball" sensors that give you the ability to tell the distance between two objects that are close together. TWO WORDS
9. What we call the cells in the epidermal layer of the skin. TWO WORDS
10. The hypodermis is also known as _____. TWO WORDS
15. A little "pocket" from which hair grows. TWO WORDS
18. A common protein that makes your skin "elastic."
19. Special cells found deep in the epidermis that produce melanin.
20. The layer of skin located below the dermis. It contains adipose tissue.
21. A tough protein found in your skin, hair and nails.
22. The place where the nail lies. TWO WORDS

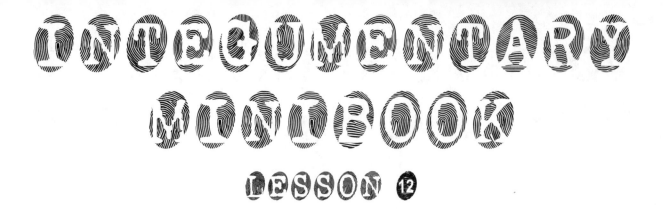

INTEGUMENTARY MINIBOOK
LESSON 12

Paste your Skin Shield
Book onto this page.

How's Your Sense of Touch?

Let's see how well your sense of touch works. Have a partner place objects in a paper bag. Now, close your eyes and reach in the bag. Can you identify what the objects are just by touching them? You can also play the game "What's in Ned's Head?" It's based on the same concept of using your sense of touch. Players race against one another to quickly and accurately find the different items placed inside Ned's Head. This fun family game can be purchased at your local toy store.

Examine Your Skin

Use a magnifying glass to study your skin up close. Do you see all the little holes in your skin? Do you see the tiny hairs? What else do you see?

Examine People's Hair

With their permission, take a strand of hair from each of your friends and family members. Try not to hurt them! Now, tape the strands to a sheet of paper and label to whom each strand belongs. Study the hairs under a magnifying glass or with a microscope. How do the strands differ? How are they the same?

Test Substances on Your Skin

Some substances stay on your skin's surface, while other substances are absorbed by your skin. Let's see what happens when you place four different substances on your skin.

You will need:
Lotion
Water
Alcohol
Oil

Make a hypothesis about what will happen to each substance when it is placed on your skin. Turn your arm upward so the inside of your arm is facing up. Now place your arm on a table in the upward position. Next, put one drop of each substance on your arm, keeping your arm very still. Watch what happens.

Crime Scene Investigation

You can purchase kits that allow you to lift fingerprints off of items (such as desks, cups, glasses, cans and such). This is a fun activity that will teach you a lot about Crime Scene Investigators. Check the Internet to find where to purchase the kits.

My Skin Projects
Lesson 12

What I did:

What I did:

What I learned:

What I learned:

SCIENTIFIC SPECULATION SHEET

Sensing Sensitivity

Lesson 12

Name_____   Date _____

Materials Used:

Procedure:

Hypothesis:

Results:

Conclusion:

Fascinating Facts

about the

Lymphatic and Immune Systems

Lesson 13

WHAT DO YOU REMEMBER?
LESSON 13

1. What is a pathogen?

2. What is a disease?

3. Name one kind of disease.

4. How do lymph nodes protect us from diseases?

5. Where can stem cells that develop into disease-fighting cells be found?

6. Name some of the systems that help keep us well as our first line of defense.

7. What name is given to that part of our immunity?

8. What does a fever do?

9. What do we call the immunity we get from cells that analyze attackers and remember them in case they come back?

10. How are antibodies formed in the body?

11. How do vaccines work?

12. How was penicillin discovered?

Lymphatic and Immune Systems
Lesson 13

Pathogens

_____   _____
_____   _____
_____   _____
_____   _____
_____   _____
_____   _____
_____   _____

Lymphatic System

_____   _____
_____   _____
_____   _____
_____   _____
_____   _____
_____   _____
_____   _____

172

Lesson 13

Immune System

Copywork

All the days ordained for me were written in your book before one of them came to be. How precious to me are your thoughts, O God! How vast is the sum of them!

Psalm 139:16-17

_____

_____

_____

_____

_____

_____

_____

Copywork

All the days ordained for me were written in your book before one of them came to be. How precious to me are your thoughts, O God! How vast is the sum of them!

Psalm 139:16-17

VOCABULARY CROSSWORD
LYMPHATIC SYSTEM

LYMPHATIC SYSTEM
LOCALIZED INFECTION
MUTATION
ACUTE
BENIGN
LYMPH NODES
SPLEEN

IMMUNITY
SYSTEMIC INFECTION
TUMOR
CHRONIC
CONTAGIOUS
LYMPH VESSELS
LYMPH

PATHOGENS
BACTERIA
DISEASE
MALIGNANT
INFECTIOUS DISEASES
TONSILS

VOCABULARY CROSSWORD
LYMPHATIC SYSTEM

Across

2. When a disease is life-threatening it is said to be _____.
6. The name of the fluid that enters the lymph vessels.
9. When a disease does not cause significant harm it is said to be _____.
11. Diseases that are caused by parasites such as bacteria, fungi, worms and viruses. TWO WORDS
12. The largest of the lymph organs. Its main job is to filter blood.
13. Microscopic germs that get inside your body and can potentially cause an infection.
14. Masses of tissue in the throat that work much like your lymph nodes.
15. What we call diseases that can be spread from one person to another.
17. Tiny masses found scattered throughout your body that filter lymph fluid. TWO WORDS
18. The body's ability to resist infection and disease.

Down

1. An infection that spreads throughout your body, affecting many of your body's systems. TWO WORDS
2. The change that happens in DNA when it is not copied correctly.
3. An infection that is restricted to one area of your body. TWO WORDS
4. The term that is used to describe diseases that are short-lived.
5. One-celled organisms found nearly everywhere on your body.
6. The vessels through which lymph fluid travels. TWO WORDS
7. Something that upsets the normal homeostatic functioning of your body's systems.
8. The part of your body's defense against infections that includes special nodes and vessels, and carries a special fluid. TWO WORDS
10. The term that is used to describe diseases that are long-lasting.
16. When a cell starts to reproduce abnormally, a _____ is formed.

VOCABULARY CROSSWORD
IMMUNE SYSTEM

LYMPHOCYTES

INNATE IMMUNITY

HISTAMINES

ADAPTIVE IMMUNITY

ALLERGIES

ACQUIRED IMMUNITY

ANTIBIOTICS

T LYMPHOCYTES

COMPLEMENT SYSTEM

PUS

ANTIBODIES

AUTOIMMUNE DISEASES

ACTIVE ARTIFICIAL IMMUNITY

INNATE

INFLAMMATION

B LYMPHOCYTES

KILLER T CELLS

PASSIVE IMMUNITY

PENICILLIN

VOCABULARY CROSSWORD
IMMUNE SYSTEM

Across

6. The swelling of tissue. It is an important part of the body's immune response.
12. Special proteins made by B cells that lock onto foreign antigens, flagging them for destruction.
14. Medicines made from chemicals. They are very effective at killing unwanted living organisms that invade our bodies.
16. Immunity that occurs when your immune system is exposed to, and responds to, a specific threat. TWO WORDS
18. Special white blood cells inside the lymph nodes.
19. Cells that are developed in the bone marrow and are trained to spot and attack foreign cells. They are also called B cells. TWO WORDS

Down

1. Immunity that is acquired without any action on the part of the body's immune system. TWO WORDS
2. The second line of your innate immunity. It is composed mostly of proteins made in the liver and causes parts of your body to become inflamed when needed. TWO WORDS
3. Special T cells that attack and destroy "flagged" cells. THREE WORDS
4. Immunity that is generated by vaccinations that stimulate the immune system in an artificial way. THREE WORDS
5. Cells that are sent to the thymus for special training in spotting and attacking foreign cells. They are also called T cells. TWO WORDS
7. Diseases in which the body forms antibodies against its own tissue. TWO WORDS
8. What we call the wide range of defenses, such as the skin barrier and inflammation, that act in the same way no matter what the attack. These are defenses you are born with, not defenses that result from a vaccination or the flu you may have had last year. TWO WORDS
9. A sophisticated system of defense that ensures your body doesn't get certain diseases more than once. TWO WORDS
10. A substance (made up of damaged tissue, living and dead bacteria and dead white blood cells) your body sometimes produces at the site of trapped bacteria.
11. Special kinds of chemicals that are released and sent to injured tissue.
13. These occur when your immune system overreacts to non-harmful substances that get inside your body.
15. The first antibiotic to be widely used. It comes from a mold.
17. The term used to describe defenses that are available to your body all the time. They respond to every threat in the same manner, such as your skin or a fever.

Defense Minibook
Lesson 13

Paste your Defense
Accordion Book onto
this page.

Participate in a Science Fair

Consider participating in a science fair with bacteria as your topic. Some possible things to study and explore are:

1. What methods are most effective in keeping a toothbrush free from bacteria?
2. Which mouthwash best fights bacteria?
3. Which cleaner is the most effective at eliminating bacteria?
4. Do any herbs inhibit bacteria growth? Which ones might?
5. Are tables at the local restaurant bacteria free?
6. How long does bacteria stay on toys?

Write a Book Report

There are many children's books on plagues, diseases, bacteria, animal bites and medicinal discoveries. Choose a topic and write a report that can be presented to your homeschool group.

Book and DVD Suggestions

Louis Pasteur: Founder of Modern Medicine by John Hudson Tiner. Focusing on the Christian character of Pasteur, this book supports the Biblical view of Creation.

Pasteur's Fight Against Microbes by Beverly Birch. This book has an abundance of beautiful illustrations and is comprehensive for elementary aged children.

An American Plague: The True and Terrifying Story of the Yellow Fever Epidemic of 1793 (Newberry Honor Book) by Jim Murphy. This powerful, dramatic account traces the devastating course of the epidemic.

Bubonic Plague by Jim Whiting. A historical account of the plague written for young elementary students.

Fever 1793 by Laurie Halse Anderson. This is a gripping story about a 14 yr. old girl who seeks to live morally amidst rampant death. The book has won many awards and is classified as Teen Middle.

What Makes You Ill? by Usborne Books. The simple text and detailed illustrations combine to answer questions related to what makes you ill. The answers are given in clear, step-by-step stages. Young readers will enjoy learning about germs and how to stay healthy.

The Germinators: The Immune System by Moody Press (Newton's Workshop Series). A fun-filled, live action DVD about the immune system. Recommended for ages 7-12. 60 minutes.

Standard Deviants School - Anatomy, Program 11 - Nutrition and Disease Prevention (Classroom Edition DVD). Discover some of the major causes of diseases, and what you can do to lower your risk of getting them.

My Lymphatic Project
Lesson 13

What I did:

What I learned:

SCIENTIFIC SPECULATION SHEET

Testing for Bacteria and Fungi

Lesson 13

Name_____   Date _____

Materials Used:

Procedure:

Hypothesis:

Results:

Conclusion:

Fascinating Facts

about

GROWTH

AND

DEVELOPMENT

LESSON 14

_____
_____
_____
_____
_____
_____
_____
_____
_____
_____
_____

_____
_____
_____
_____
_____
_____
_____
_____
_____
_____
_____

_____
_____
_____
_____
_____

WHAT DO YOU REMEMBER?
LESSON 14

1. How do cells divide?

2. At what point were you alive when you were in your mother's womb?

3. How many chromosomes do people have?

4. What is a trait?

5. What are genes?

6. Where is your DNA located?

7. What is mitosis?

8. What is meiosis?

9. What are gametes?

10. Who was Gregor Mendel?

11. What makes humans different from animals?

12. What are the two main reasons we said you shouldn't believe humans evolved from apes?

13. Who were the cavemen?

14. Why did God create you?

Possible Purpose Page
Ephesians 2:10

My Strengths, Gifts and Talents

_____
_____
_____
_____
_____
_____
_____
_____
_____
_____
_____

My Interests

_____
_____
_____
_____
_____
_____
_____
_____
_____
_____
_____

How I can Glorify God with my Life

_____
_____
_____
_____

Copywork

"For you formed my inward parts;
You wove me in my mother's
womb.

Psalm 139:13

_____

_____

_____

_____

_____

_____

Copywork

"For you formed my inward parts;
You wove me in my mother's womb.
Psalm 139:13

VOCABULARY CROSSWORD GROWTH AND DEVELOPMENT

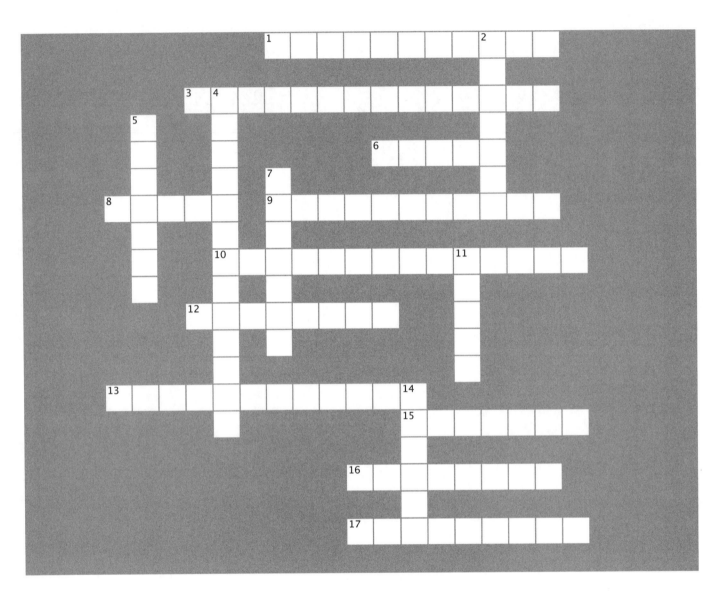

EMBRYO

AMNIOTIC SAC

FETUS

PUBERTY

GENETICS

TRAIT

GENES

HEREDITY

CHROMOSOMES

MITOSIS

MEIOSIS

GAMETES

FRATERNAL TWINS

IDENTICAL TWINS

DOMINANT GENE

RECESSIVE GENE

EVOLUTION

VOCABULARY CROSSWORD GROWTH AND DEVELOPMENT

Across

1. Your DNA is stored in these 46 compact units.
3. Babies that develop in the womb together but are made from different gametes, possessing different DNA. TWO WORDS
6. What you were called when you were developing in your mother's womb after your first two months of life.
8. The parts of your DNA that determine certain characteristics or traits. They were passed down to you from your biological parents.
9. The fluid-filled bag in which the embryo lives. It is attached to the mother. TWO WORDS
10. Babies that develop in the womb together and are made from the same gametes, possessing the same DNA. TWO WORDS
12. The study of genes and heredity.
13. A gene that will determine a trait, regardless of what trait the corresponding gene encodes. TWO WORDS
15. The process whereby a cell divides to make two new cells with exactly the same DNA as the original cell.
16. The passing on of traits from parents to their children.
17. The false idea that man developed over millions of years, gradually changing from a single-cell organism to an ape to a human being.

Down

2. A special cell division process that results in unique cells called gametes (they have half the regular number of chromosomes).
4. A gene that is "sleeping." The trait encoded on this gene will be masked if paired with a dominant gene. TWO WORDS
5. The period between the ages of nine and fourteen when the human body begins taking on a more adult form, and the differences between males and females become more obvious.
7. Male or female reproductive cells that combine to produce a single cell that develops into a new life.
11. A recognizable physical characteristic, like eye color, skin color, or hair texture.
14. What you were called when you were developing in your mother's womb during your first two months of life.

GROWTH AND DEVELOPMENT MINIBOOK
LESSON 14

Paste your Growth and
Development Fan onto
this page.

Create a Time Line

If you have visited the same pediatrician for many years, he or she will have a record of your growth. You can ask the receptionist at your pediatrician's office for a copy of your growth charts (some will charge a small fee), and you can create a time line of your growth over the years.

You can also create a time line of your development by charting the ages at which you developed certain skills, such as: walking, talking, learning to read, riding a bike and such.

Another idea is to make a time line of your family. Search the Internet to find examples of time lines.

Make a Genetic Family Tree

Most family trees simply list names of family members. You can create your own family tree and make it really special by listing a unique trait for each family member. You can choose physical traits or character traits, or both! Do you see any similarities between family members? Which family member are you most like?

Study Genetics:
Wisconsin Fast Plants Study on Genetics: Hairy's Inheritance: Competing to Make the Hairiest Plant Kit

Here's a fun, competitive activity that will help you learn about genetics. During this study, you'll be competing to make the hairiest plant, so find a friend and let the competition begin! Each week you'll do an activity that focuses on raising and crossbreeding fast plants, with the goal of breeding an unusually hairy plant. Through this study, you'll learn a great deal about botany and caring for plants. You'll also explore pollination and will come to understand hybrid plants and many other scientific concepts related to genetics.

Book and DVD Suggestions

Gene Machines by Frances R. Balkwill and Mic Rolph. This book has one major flaw: the authors are seeking to indoctrinate students in evolutionary thought. They make a big deal over the number of genes humans have compared to other animals, and also how similar human organ systems are to those of mice. But you can avoid those discussions by skipping pages 20-23, unless you are prepared to discuss how similar design does not indicate a common ancestor, but a common Designer!

Gregor Mendel: The Friar Who Grew Peas by Cheryl Bardoe. A wonderful gem, with beautiful illustrations and a great story line unraveling DNA and genetics.

The Bible (Genesis chapter 30). Read the story of how Jacob tricked Laban by crossbreeding goats.

The Wonders of God's Creation: Human Life (Moody). In this DVD you'll learn about the Master Creator as you take a journey deep into the human body.

My Growth and Developmenopment Project
Lesson 14

What I did:

What I learned:

Name _____   Date _____

Final Review Questions

1. What did God ask the Hebrews to do that we now know protects people from illness?

2. Draw a cell below and label as many parts as you can remember.

3. What is an important mineral the body needs to make bones that are strong and healthy?

4. What do bones manufacture in the red bone marrow?

5. What are some ways to make your bones strong?

6. Where are the smallest bones in your body located?

7. Which is the longest bone in your body?

8. What are phalanges?

9. What are the muscles called that are attached to your skeleton and move your arms, legs and other body parts?

10. What is the connective tissue called that attaches your muscles to your bones?

11. What nutrient must you eat to make your muscles strong and healthy?

12. What is the muscle called that makes up your heart muscle?

13. How is saliva helpful to your body?

14. What does stomach acid do?

15. Name the three parts of the small intestine.

16. What does the renal system do?

17. What is a vitamin deficiency?

18. How does one get all the vitamins and minerals they need?

19. Name at least three of the organs that make up the respiratory system.

20. What does the mucus layer in your nose do?

21. What are the two tubes that lead from your trachea to your lungs called?

22. What are the balloon-like sacs inside the lungs (which allow oxygen to pass into your bloodstream) called?

23. What is the name of the life-saving method that enables people to compress the abdomen and expel air from the lungs to dislodge something that is causing a person to choke?

24. What is the name of the thin sheet of muscle that is mostly responsible for your breathing?

25. Which system contains your arteries, veins and heart?

26. What powers the movement of blood from your heart to the rest of your body?

27. How does one grow more capillaries?

28. How does having more capillaries help your body?

29. What is the name of the liquid in which your blood cells float?

30. Which blood cells carry hemoglobin and iron?

31. What is the condition that occurs when a person does not have an adequate number of red blood cells in his body (often due to not eating enough iron)?

32. Which blood cells travel around the blood stream looking for germs and other waste products?

33. What is the name of the cell fragments in the blood that enable your blood to clot?

34. Where is your blood made?

35. The right atrium receives (oxygenated   deoxygenated) blood. Circle one.

36. The left atrium receives (oxygenated   deoxygenated) blood. Circle one.

37. Label the cerebrum, cerebellum and brain stem on the drawing here.

38. What are the cells that carry messages to and from your brain called?

39. Name the two parts of the central nervous system (CNS).

40. The somatic nervous system is responsible for (voluntary   involuntary) movement. Circle one.

41. The autonomic nervous system is responsible for (voluntary   involuntary) movement. Circle one.

42. What does the olfactory system allow you to do?

43. Name the three bones found in the middle ear.

44. What is the name of the rod and cone containing layer of your inner eye, onto which the images you look at are projected?

45. What does the integumentary system include?

46. What are pathogens?

47. What are some things God gave the human body as defenses against disease?

48. What is it called when a cell divides, making an exact copy of itself?

49. What is it called when one cell divides to form four totally different cells?

50. Why did God make you?

VOCABULARY CROSSWORD SOLUTIONS

Lesson 1: Introduction to Anatomy and Physiology

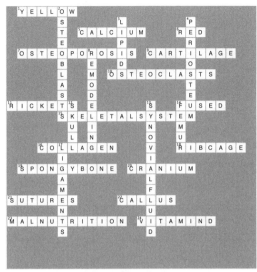

Lesson 2: The Skeletal System

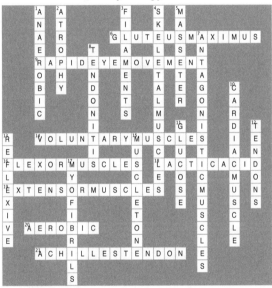

Lesson 3: The Muscular System

Lesson 4: The Digestive System

Lesson 4: The Digestive and Renal Systems

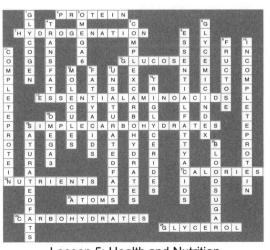

Lesson 5: Health and Nutrition

197

VOCABULARY CROSSWORD SOLUTIONS

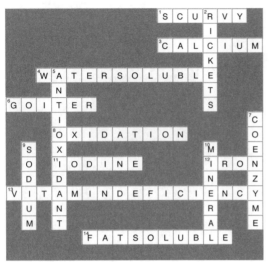

Lesson 5: Vitamins

Lesson 6: The Respiratory System

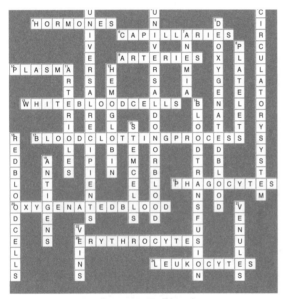

Lesson 7: Blood

Lesson 8: The Cardiovascular System

Lesson 9: The Nervous System

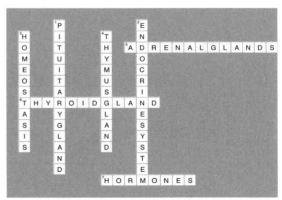

Lesson 9: The Endocrine System

198

VOCABULARY CROSSWORD SOLUTIONS

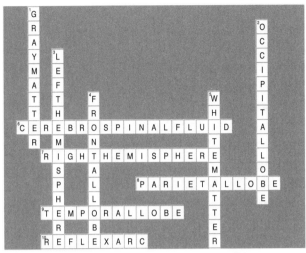

Lesson 10: The Nervous System Extended

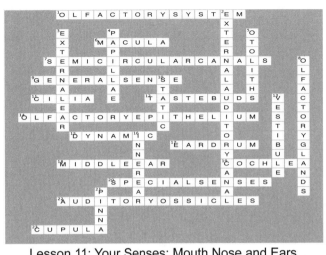

Lesson 11: Your Senses: Mouth Nose and Ears

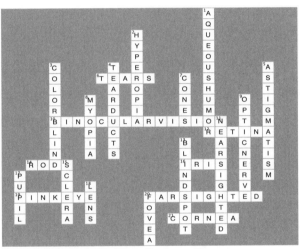

Lesson 11: Your Senses: Eyes

Lesson 12: The Integumentary System

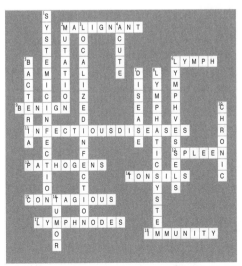

Lesson 13: The Lymphatic System

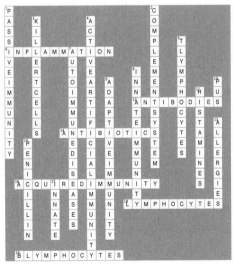

Lesson 13: The Immune System

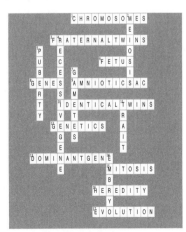

Lesson 14: Growth and Development

199

Name _____ Date_____

Final Review Solutions

1. Answers will vary: eat only clean animals, do not drink blood, do not eat animal fat, wash your hands.
2.

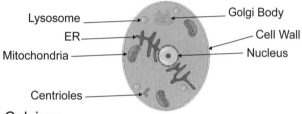

3. Calcium
4. Red blood cells
5. Answers will vary: get calcium, get exercise, get vitamin D
6. In the ear
7. Femur (upper leg bone)
8. Bones in the fingers and toes
9. Skeletal muscles
10. Tendons
11. Protein
12. Cardiac muscle
13. It helps digest food, makes food taste better, contains chemicals that protect your teeth, and defends your mouth from infection.
14. Either answer is correct: kills bacteria or breaks down the food (protein) you eat into smaller chemicals to be absorbed by your body.
15. Duodenum, jejunum, ileum
16. Produces urine waste to be eliminated from the body
17. An illness which occurs when people do not get the proper amounts of vitamins needed to be healthy
18. By eating a varied diet with many different kinds of foods
19. Answers will vary: nose, trachea, bronchi, lungs, diaphragm
20. Answers will vary: catches dust and other particles suspended in the air so they do not go into the lungs, allows airborne chemicals to dissolve so they can be detected, moisturizes the air
21. Bronchi
22. Alveoli

23. Heimlich maneuver
24. Diaphragm
25. Circulatory system
26. The heart pumping
27. By exercising
28. It lowers your blood pressure and makes it easier for your heart to work.
29. Plasma
30. Red blood cells or erythrocytes
31. Anemia
32. White blood cells or leukocytes
33. Platelets
34. Inside the red bone marrow or inside the bones
35. Deoxygenated
36. Oxygenated
37.

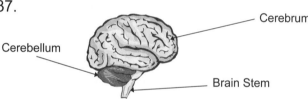

38. Neurons
39. Brain and spinal cord
40. Voluntary
41. Involuntary
42. Smell
43. Malleus, incus and stapes (anvil, hammer and stirrup)
44. Retina
45. Skin and hair
46. Germs, or any of the following: bacteria, viruses, fungi, parasites
47. Answers will vary: skin, immune system, lymphatic system, white blood cells, lymph nodes, T cells, B cells, antibodies, antigens, vaccinations, antibiotics
48. Mitosis
49. Meiosis
50. Answers will vary: to bring glory to God, to experience joy in my relationship with Him both here and in heaven, to use my gifts and talents for God

MY ANATOMY FIELD TRIP

Place: Date:

The purpose of this field trip:

What I saw/did on this trip:

What I learned:

My favorite part:

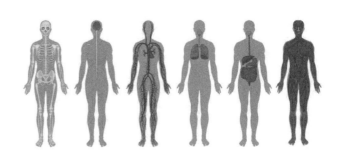

MY ANATOMY FIELD TRIP

Place: Date:

The purpose of this field trip:

What I saw/did on this trip:

What I learned:

My favorite part:

CREATION CONFIRMATION MINIBOOK

(Instructions on back)

Creation
Confirmation

Creation
Confirmation

Creation
Confirmation

It's important to remember all you've learned about God and Creation in this course. This Creation Confirmation Minibook will enable you to record and recall your learning.

Instructions:
1. Cut out the Creation Confirmation Minibook cover and rectangles on pages A1 and A3 along the dotted lines. **Do not cut the gold fold lines!**
2. Fold the pages along the gold lines.
3. Place the pages inside the Anatomy cover of the book.
4. Open the book to the middle and staple it along the center.
5. As you work through each lesson of the anatomy course, write down what you learn about God, the Bible and Creation.
6. Keep your Creation Confirmation Minibook inside your anatomy book as a bookmark and a reminder to write down the things you learn about God.

Creation Confirmation Minibook

Creation Confirmation Minibook

EXTRA MINIATURE BOOKS

Here are a few extra miniature books for you to use.

Cut out the miniature books, but do not cut the black fold lines! Record any additional information you've learned about anatomy not included in the other miniature books. Fold your books and glue the back covers of the books onto the paste page of the topic you have written about.

Glue this side of the book to your paste page.

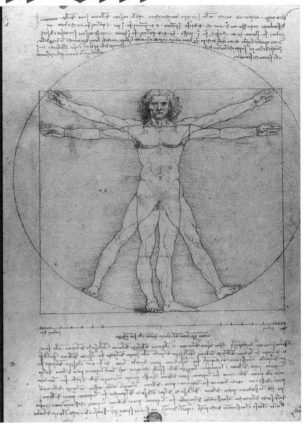

Glue this side of the book to your paste page.

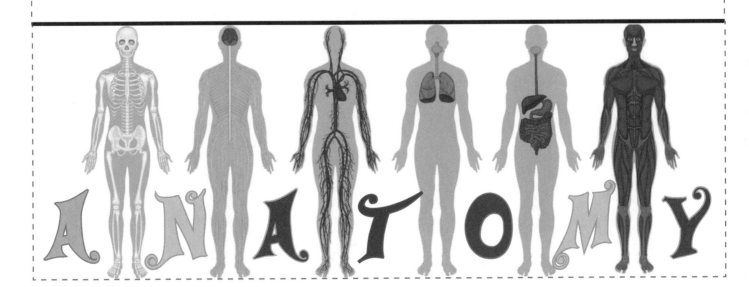

CELL WHEEL

Instructions:

1. Cut out the Cell Circle and the Fact Circle. Be sure to cut out the white empty spaces in the Cell Circle.
2. Place the Cell Circle on top of the Fact Circle, and insert a brass fastener in the center (on the gold spot) to secure the two circles.
3. On the triangle opposite each title, write what that organelle does or draw a picture of it.
4. Dab glue on the bottom of the Fact Circle and glue your Cell Wheel onto the "Cell Minibook" paste page *(NJ p. 26)*.
5. Turn the Cell Circle around to reveal the different facts about each topic.

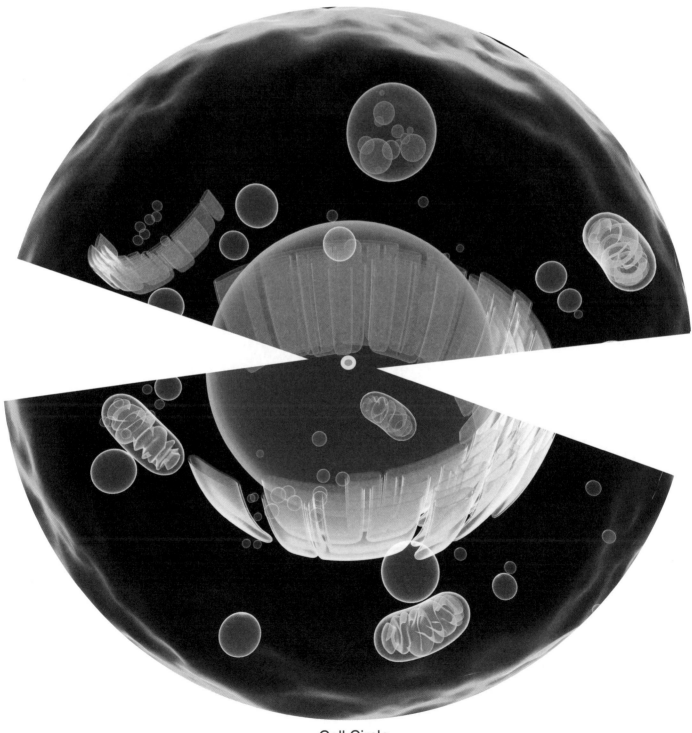

Cell Circle

Fact Circle

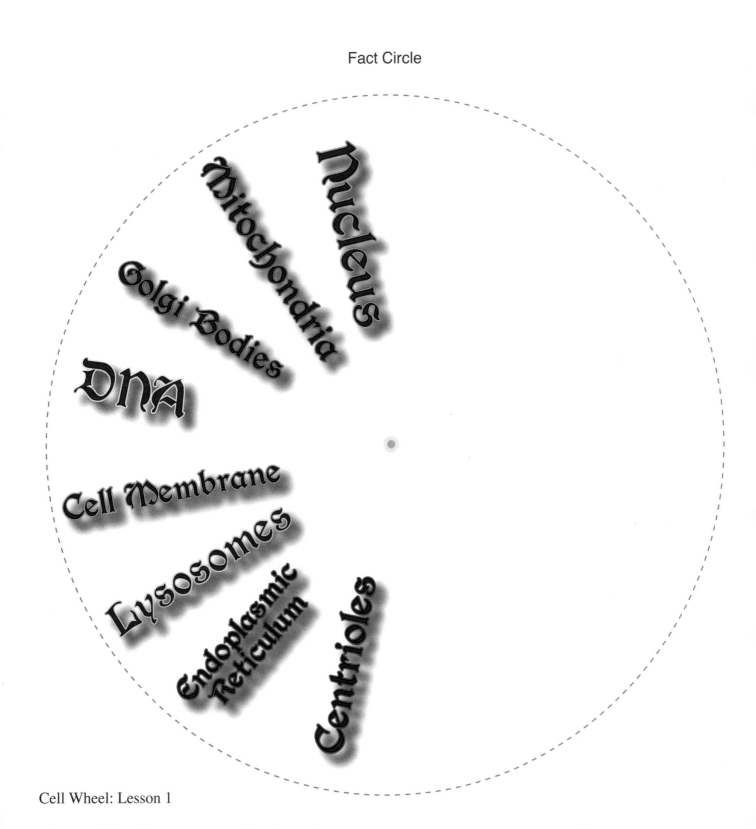

Nucleus

Mitochondria

Golgi Bodies

DNA

Cell Membrane

Lysosomes

Endoplasmic Reticulum

Centrioles

Cell Wheel: Lesson 1

Glue this side to your paste page.

Cell Wheel: Lesson 1

SKELETAL SYSTEM SHUTTER BOOK

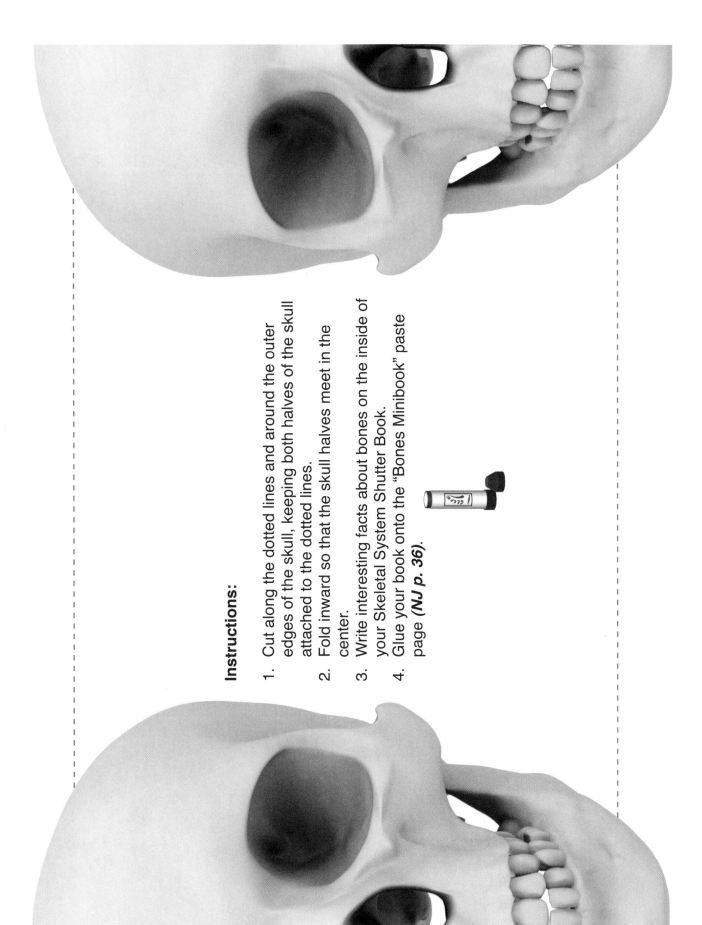

Instructions:

1. Cut along the dotted lines and around the outer edges of the skull, keeping both halves of the skull attached to the dotted lines.

2. Fold inward so that the skull halves meet in the center.

3. Write interesting facts about bones on the inside of your Skeletal System Shutter Book.

4. Glue your book onto the "Bones Minibook" paste page *(NJ p. 36)*.

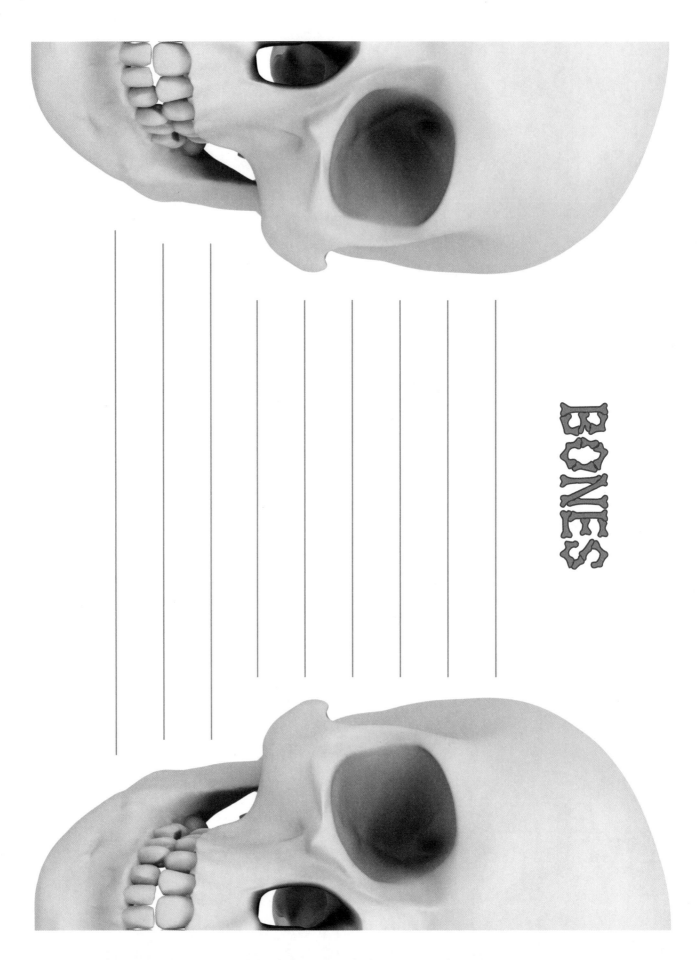

BONES

MUSCULAR SYSTEM FLAP BOOK

What are Tendons?

Describe Muscle Cells.

How do Muscles Grow?

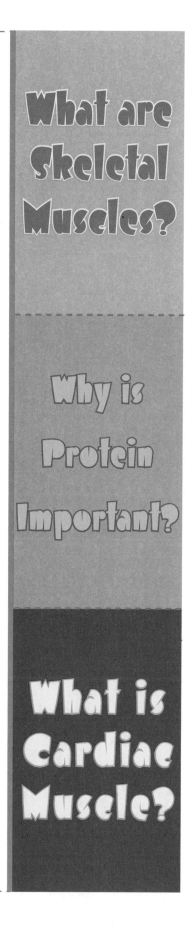

What are Skeletal Muscles?

Why is Protein Important?

What is Cardiac Muscle?

Instructions:

1. Cut out the large rectangle on this page along the dotted lines.
2. Cut between the colored rectangles along the four dotted lines that divide the rectangles. **Do not cut into the orange fold lines!**
3. Fold the colored rectangles away from you along the orange fold lines.
4. Turn over your Muscular System Flap Book and lift the flaps.
5. Write the information requested about the topics on the flaps.
6. Glue this side (with these words) to your "Muscles Minibook" paste page *(NJ p. 48)*.

Muscular System Flap Book: Lesson 3

More Muscle Facts

_____
_____
_____
_____
_____

_____
_____

_____

_____

_____

_____

_____

_____

_____
_____
_____
_____
_____
_____
_____

_____

_____

_____

_____

_____

_____

_____

_____

_____

DIGESTION POCKET

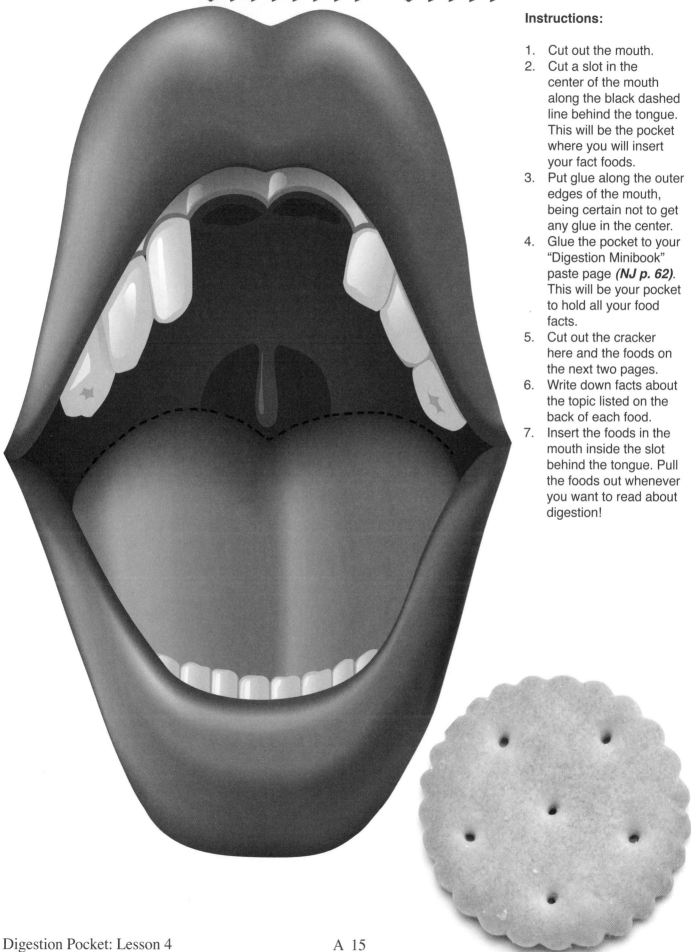

Instructions:

1. Cut out the mouth.
2. Cut a slot in the center of the mouth along the black dashed line behind the tongue. This will be the pocket where you will insert your fact foods.
3. Put glue along the outer edges of the mouth, being certain not to get any glue in the center.
4. Glue the pocket to your "Digestion Minibook" paste page *(NJ p. 62)*. This will be your pocket to hold all your food facts.
5. Cut out the cracker here and the foods on the next two pages.
6. Write down facts about the topic listed on the back of each food.
7. Insert the foods in the mouth inside the slot behind the tongue. Pull the foods out whenever you want to read about digestion!

Saliva Facts

_____

_____

_____

_____

Tooth Diagram

Label the Teeth

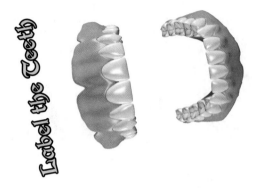

Intestine Facts

_____

_____

_____

ALIMENTARY CANAL

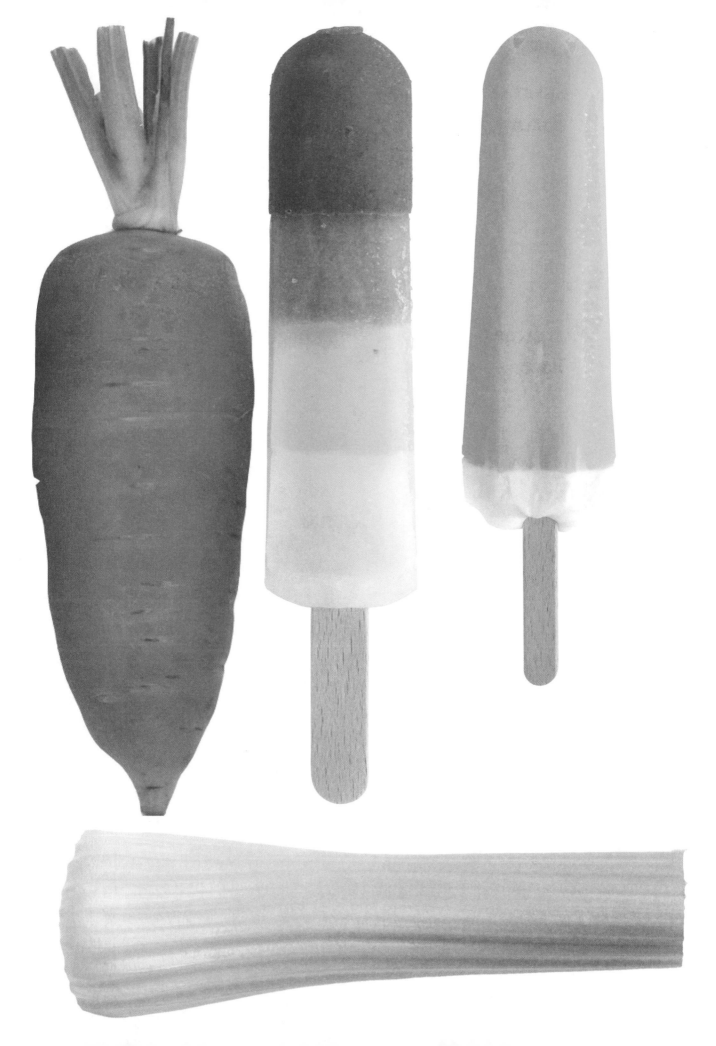

Liver
Facts

Mechanical
Digestion

Chemical
Digestion

Digestion
Facts

Pancreas
Facts

Bolus

_____

_____

_____

_____

Chyme

_____

_____

A 20

Stomach Facts

NUTRITION MATCHBOOK

This is the matchbook cover that will hold all your rectangular pages.

Instructions:

1. Cut out the matchbook cover along the dotted lines. **Do not cut the blue fold lines!**
2. Fold along the blue lines so that the large foods flap and the small cherries flap face outward in the same direction.
3. Cut out the rectangles on this page and the next and fill in the information you learned about each topic.
4. Lift the large flap and place all the pages you created under the small flap.
5. With the large cover flap open and your pages under the small flap, staple your matchbook on the white line that crosses the center of the small flap. This will hold all your pages inside. **Do not staple the cover closed!**
6. Fold the large flap down and tuck it into the small flap, like a matchbook.
7. Glue this side (with these words) onto the "Nutrition Minibook" paste page *(NJ p. 78)*.

Nutrition Matchbook: Lesson 5

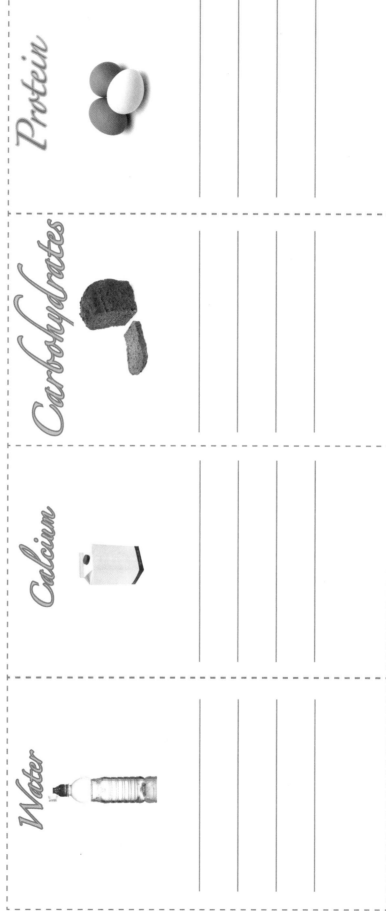

A 21

Vitamin C

Fats

Vitamin A

Vitamins D & K

B Vitamins

Minerals

RESPIRATORY MINIBOOKS

Instructions:

1. Cut out the Respiratory Mini Books along the dotted lines. **Do not cut the yellow fold lines!**
2. Fold the books along the yellow lines so the images are on the outside of the books.
3. Write facts you learned about the parts of the respiratory system listed on each book.
4. Glue your minibooks onto the "Respiratory Minibooks" paste page *(NJ p. 90)*.

Glue this side of the book to your paste page.

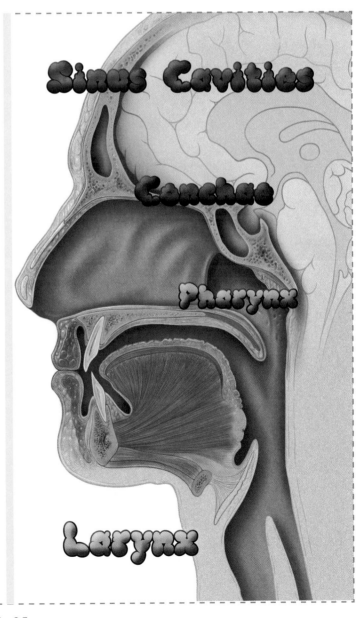

Glue this side of the book to your
paste page.

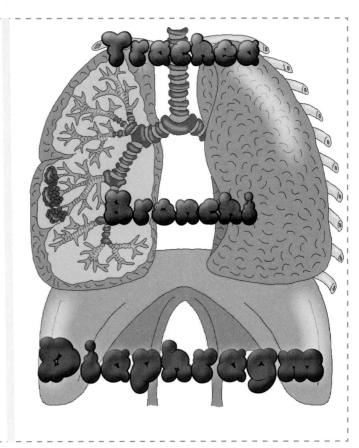

Glue this side of the book to your
paste page.

Trachea

_____

_____

Bronchi

_____

_____

Diaphragm

_____

_____

Alveoli

_____

_____

_____

Respiratory Minibooks: Lesson 6

BLOOD SHUTTER BOOKS

Instructions:

1. Cut out the four Blood Shutter Books on this page and the next. **Do not cut the gold fold lines!**
2. Fold the flaps of the books inward along the gold fold lines.
3. Open the flaps and write what you learned about blood on the insides of the books.
4. Glue your Blood Shutter Books onto the "Blood Minibooks" paste page *(NJ p. 102)*.

Blood Shutter Books: Lesson 7

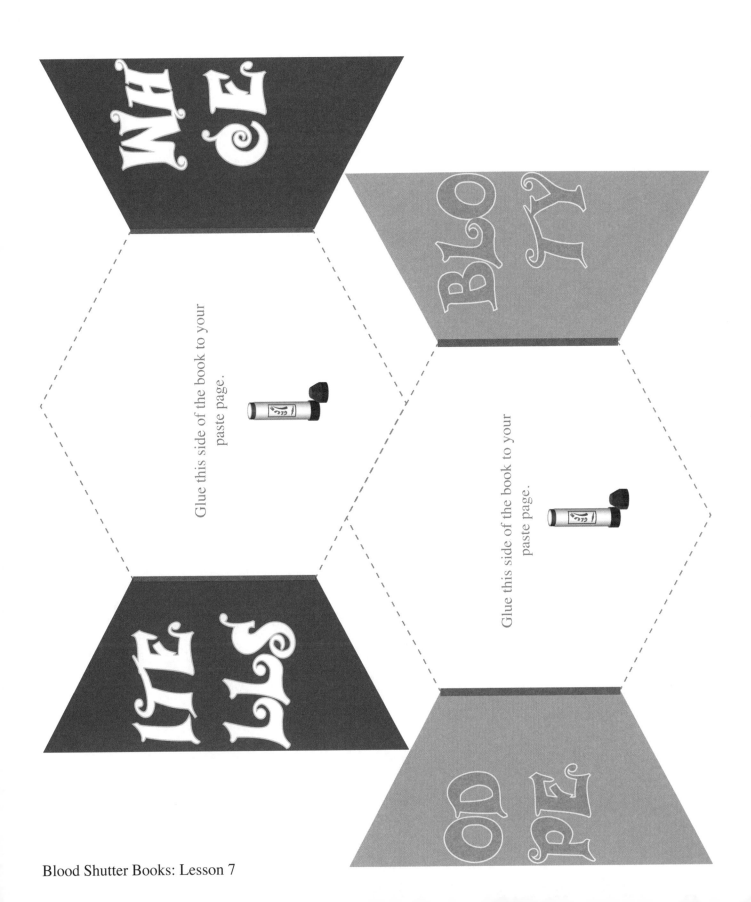

Glue this side of the book to your paste page.

Glue this side of the book to your paste page.

Blood Shutter Books: Lesson 7

CARDIO TUCK IN ENVELOPES

Instructions:

1. Cut out each Tuck In Envelope along the dotted lines. **Do not cut the red fold lines!**
2. Fold the books inward along the red fold lines to resemble an envelope.

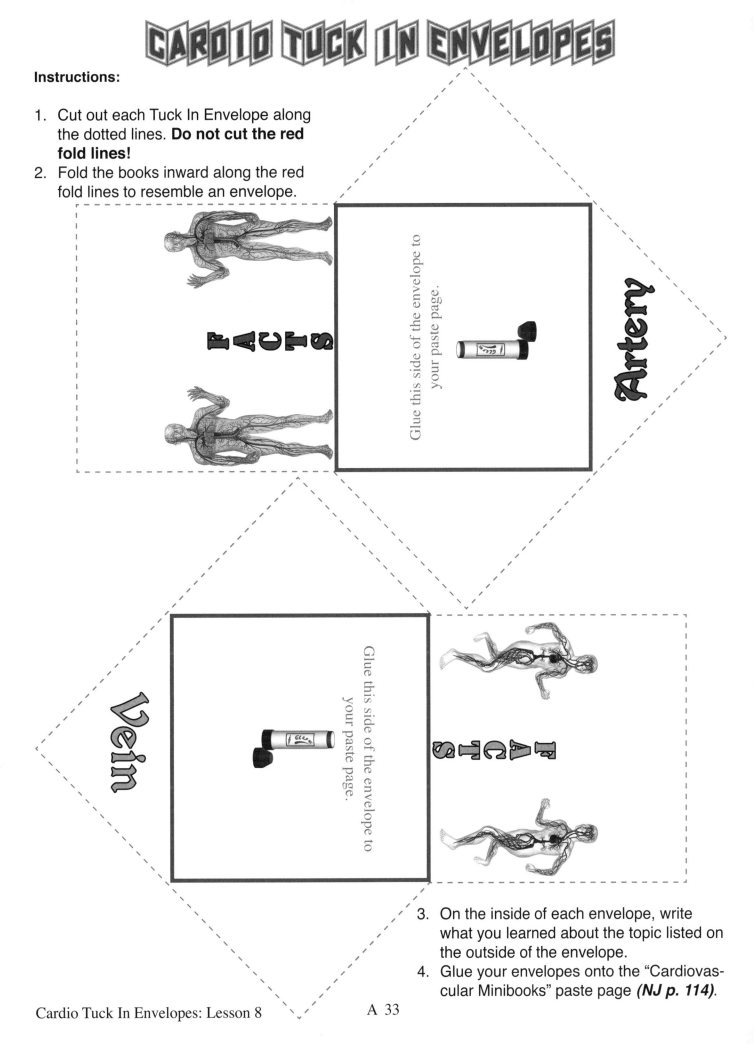

FACTS

Glue this side of the envelope to your paste page.

Artery

Vein

Glue this side of the envelope to your paste page.

FACTS

3. On the inside of each envelope, write what you learned about the topic listed on the outside of the envelope.
4. Glue your envelopes onto the "Cardiovascular Minibooks" paste page *(NJ p. 114)*.

A 34

Cardio Tuck In Envelopes: Lesson 8

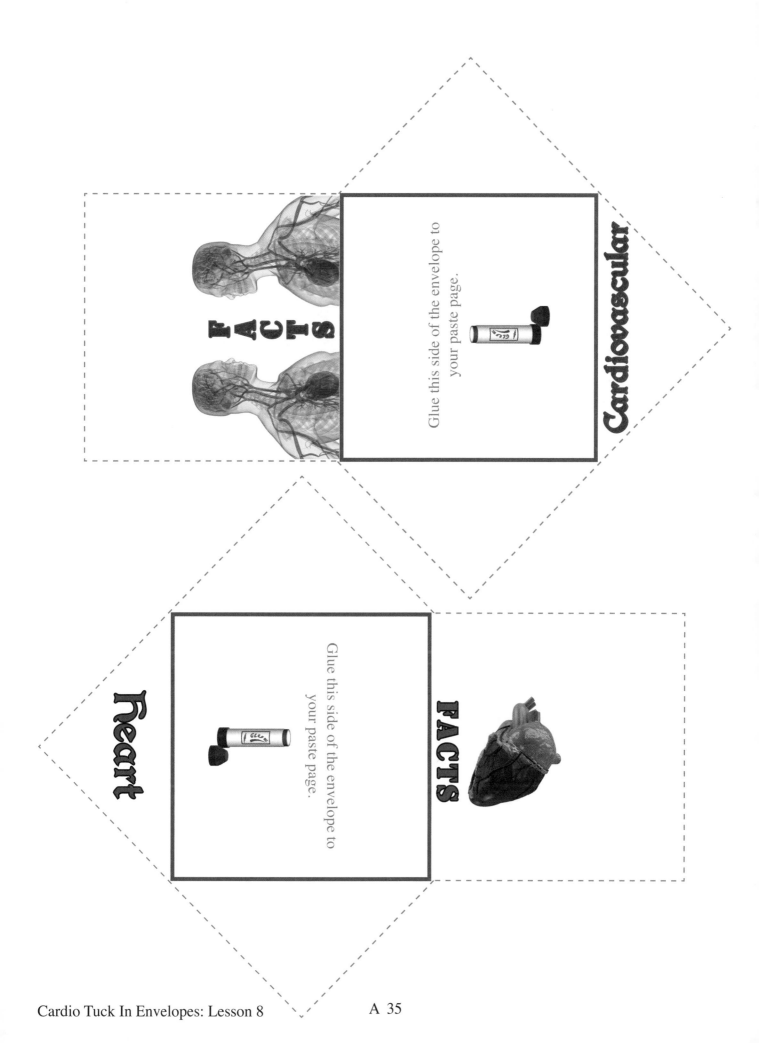

Glue this side of the envelope to your paste page.

FACTS

Cardiovascular

Glue this side of the envelope to your paste page.

Heart

FACTS

Cardio Tuck In Envelopes: Lesson 8

NERVOUS SYSTEM LAYERED BOOK

Instructions:

1. Write down facts you learned under each title listed on the rectangle pages of your layered book.
2. Cut out the four pages and the title page along the dotted lines.
3. Stack the pages on top of each other with the smallest title page on top.
4. Line the pages up at the top with the title of each page showing at the bottom.
5. Staple the pages along the top to secure them together.
6. Glue your layered book onto the "Nervous System Minibook" paste page *(NJ p. 129)*.
7. Lift the layers to read about the nervous system.

CENTRAL NERVOUS SYSTEM

_____

_____

_____

_____

CNS

PERIPHERAL NERVOUS SYSTEM

_____

_____

_____

_____

_____

PNS

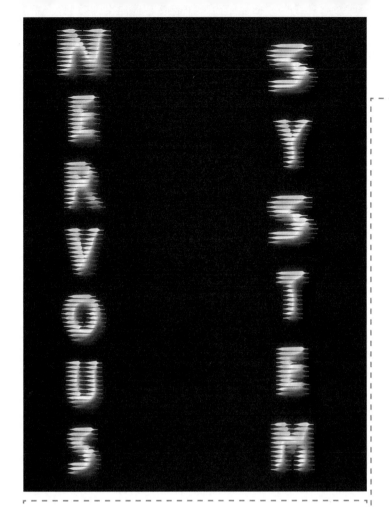

NERVOUS SYSTEM

AUTONOMIC NERVOUS SYSTEM

_____

_____

_____

_____

SOMATIC NERVOUS SYSTEM

_____

_____

_____

ANS - SNS

DRAW AND LABEL A NEURON

NEURONS

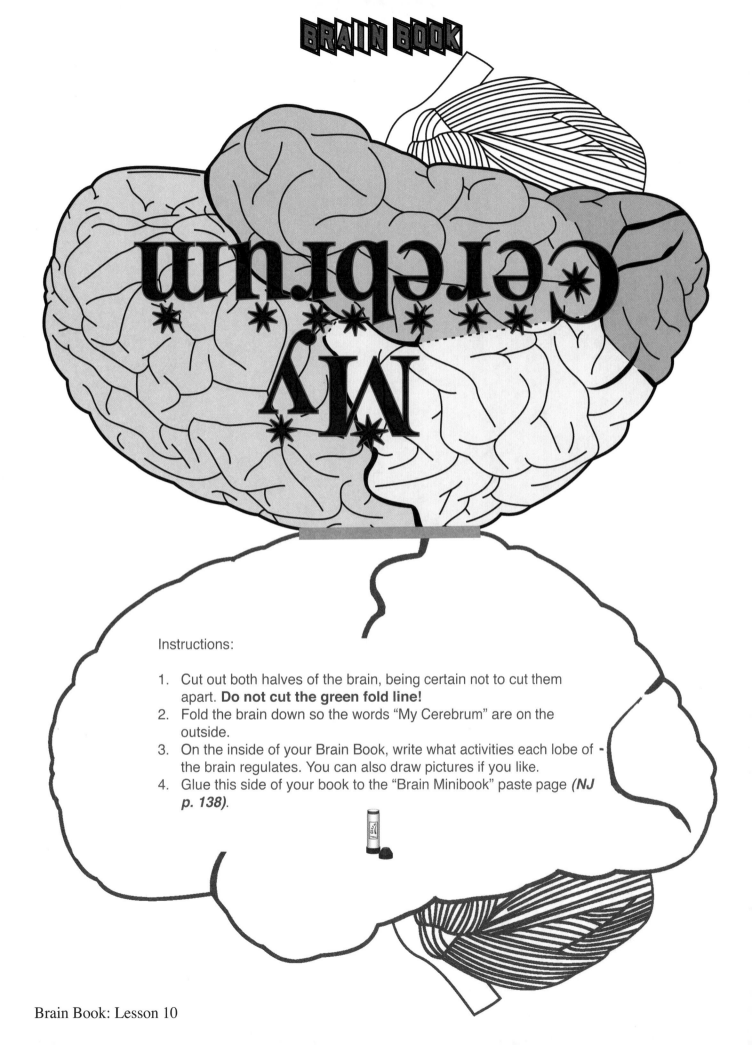

BRAIN BOOK

My Cerebrum

Instructions:

1. Cut out both halves of the brain, being certain not to cut them apart. **Do not cut the green fold line!**
2. Fold the brain down so the words "My Cerebrum" are on the outside.
3. On the inside of your Brain Book, write what activities each lobe of the brain regulates. You can also draw pictures if you like.
4. Glue this side of your book to the "Brain Minibook" paste page *(NJ p. 138)*.

Brain Book: Lesson 10

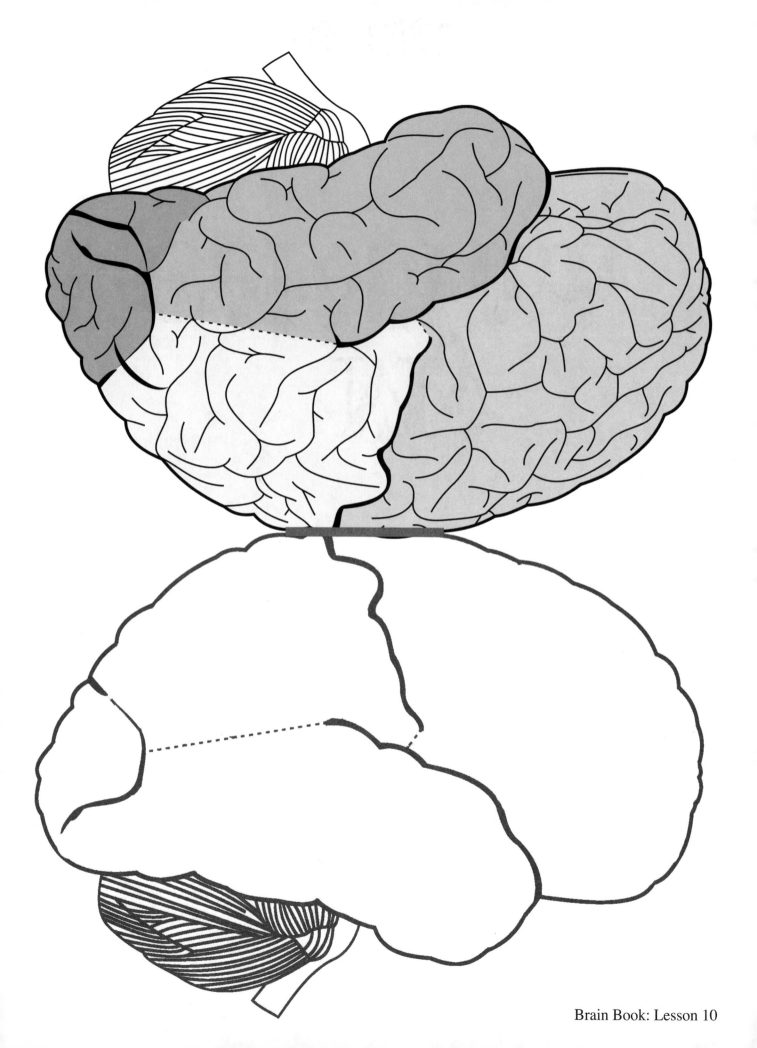

FIVE SENSES TAB BOOK

Instructions:

1. Cut out the tabbed rectangles on this and the next two pages. Fold the green cover page along the yellow fold line.
2. Fold the smell and balance page along the yellow fold line so the word "smell" is on the outside when folded. Place this page inside the green cover page.
3. Fold the taste and hearing page along the yellow line so the word "taste" is on the outside. Place the page in the center of the book so the tabs line up down the side of the book when it is closed.
4. Open the book and staple it down the center by inserting a stapler across half the book.
5. Write or draw what you learned about your senses on the pages of your book. Be sure to label the diagrams.
6. Glue your Five Senses Tab Book onto your "Senses Minibook" paste page *(NJ p. 150)*.

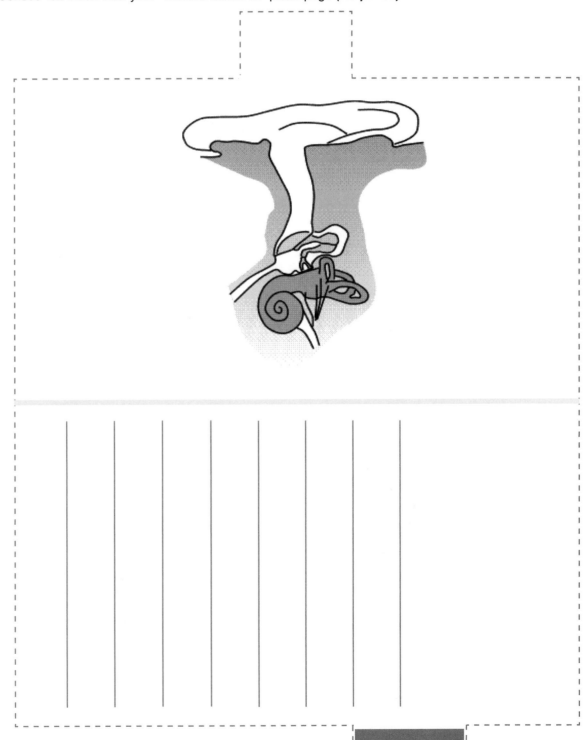

Taste

Five Senses Tab Book: Lesson 11   A 43

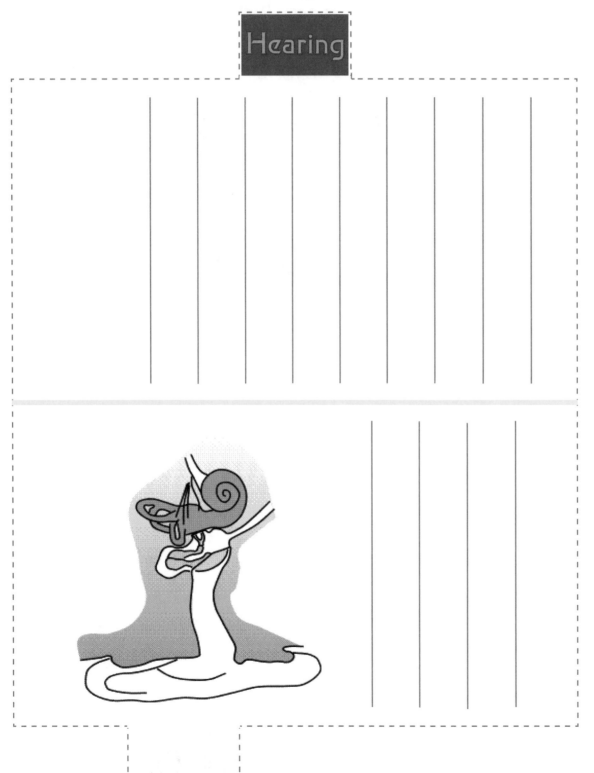

Hearing

A 44

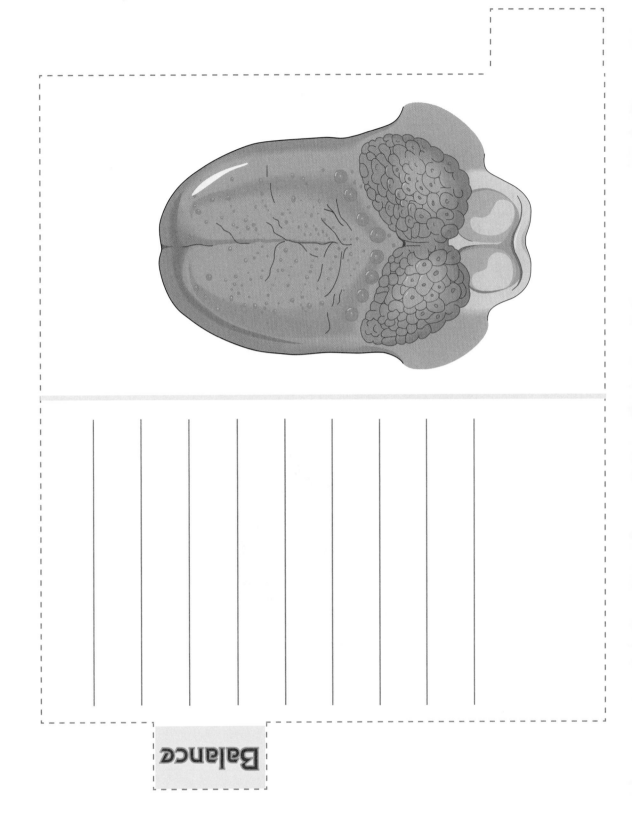

Balance

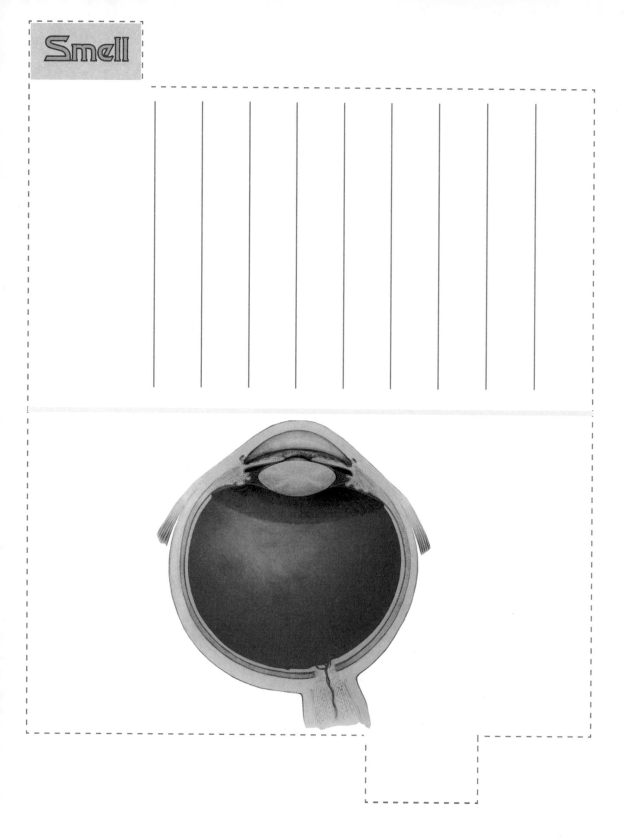

Five Senses Tab Book: Lesson 11

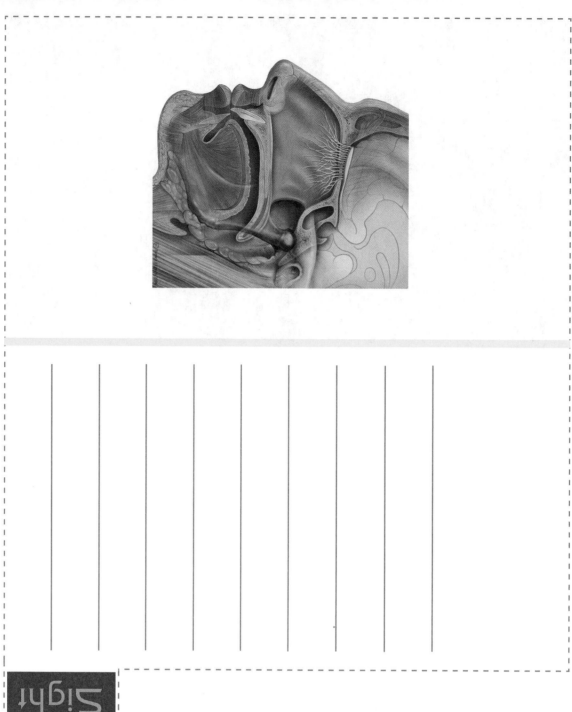

Sight

SKIN SHIELD BOOK

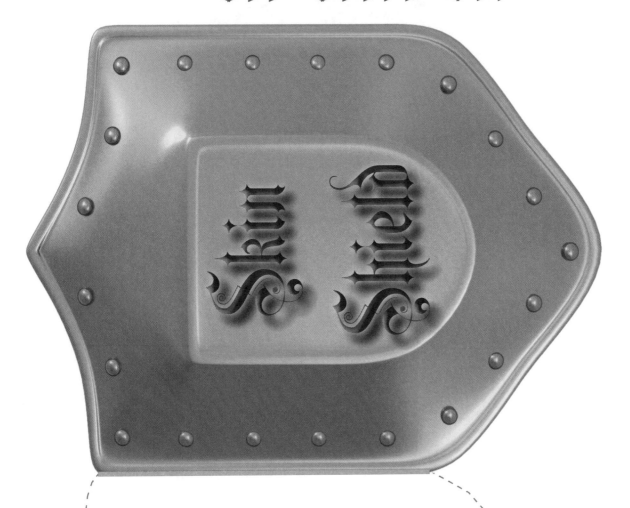

Instructions:

1. Cut out this shield book cover and the book pages along the dotted lines. **Do not cut the blue fold lines!**
2. Fold the cover and pages, inserting the pages inside the cover of the book.
3. Open the book flat. Using a stapler, reach into the center of the book and staple along the fold line to secure the pages to the cover page of the book.
4. Write information you learned about the integumentary system on the pages.
5. Glue your Skin Shield Book onto your "Integumentary Minibook" paste page *(NJ p. 166)*.

Skin Shield Book: Lesson 12

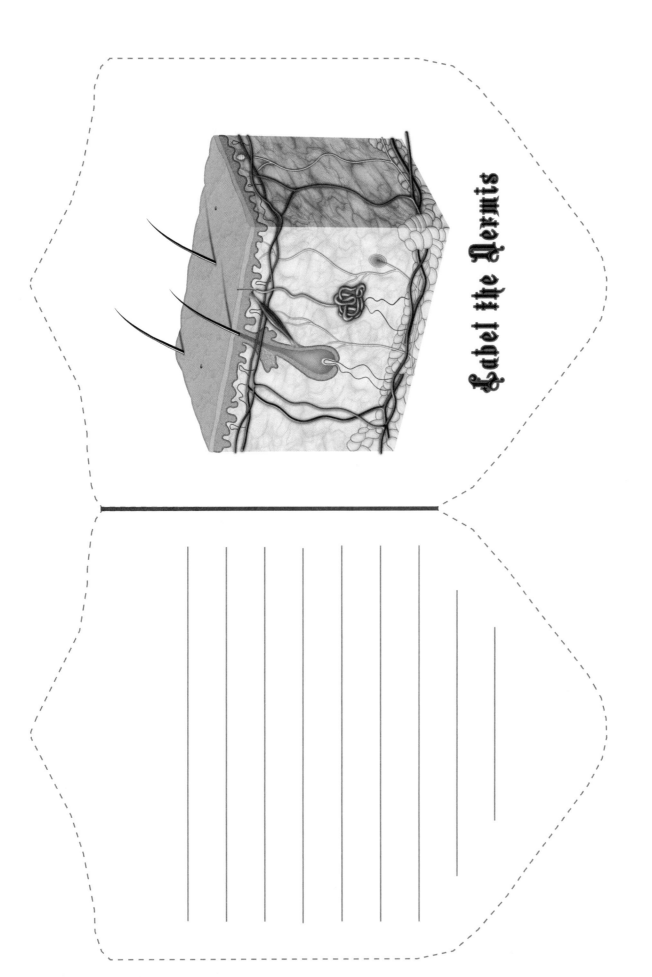

Label the Dermis

DEFENSE ACCORDION BOOK

Instructions:

1. Cut out the two halves of the Defense Accordion Book, being sure to keep the top and bottom parts of the knight attached to the paper strips. The bottom half is on the backside of this page. **Be sure not to cut the blue fold lines!**
2. Glue the bottom half of the knight to the top half by putting glue on the glue tab and affixing it to the back of the immunity box.
3. Write what you learned about our amazing defense system under the topics listed on the paper strip.
4. Fold the long strip accordion style along the blue fold lines.
5. Glue the back of the knight's shoulders onto the "Defense Mini-book" paste page *(NJ p. 180)*.

DEFENSE SYSTEMS

BAD GUYS

LYMPHATIC SYSTEM

IMMUNITY

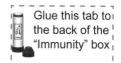
Glue this tab to
the back of the
"Immunity" box

B & T LYMPHOCYTES

_____

_____

_____

_____

ANTIBODIES

_____

_____

_____

_____

ANTIBIOTICS

_____

_____

_____

GROWTH AND DEVELOPMENT FAN

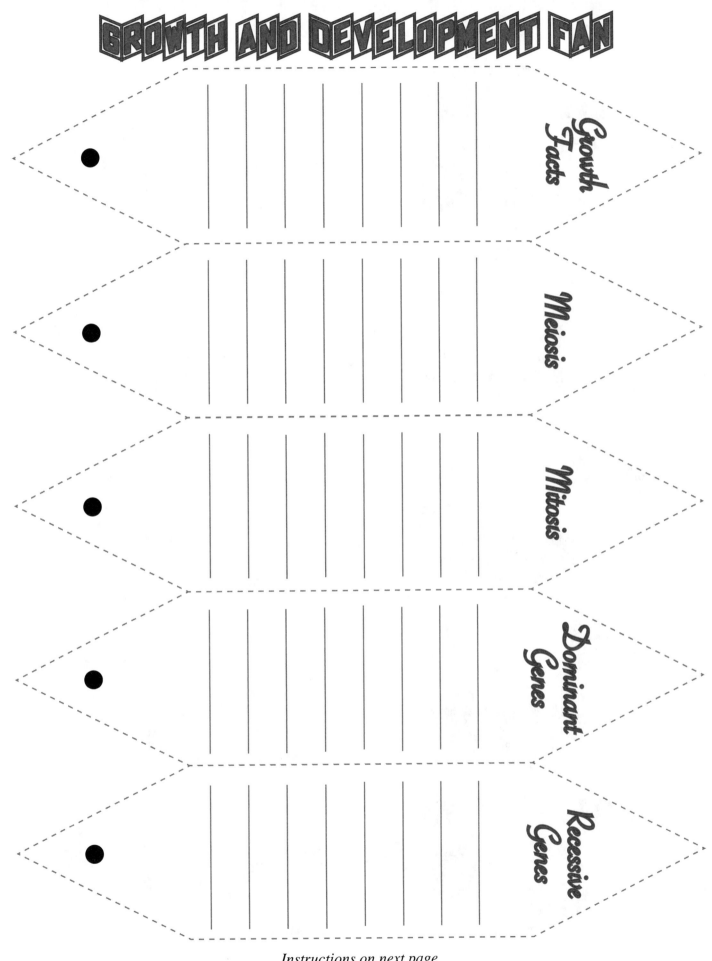

Growth Facts

Meiosis

Mitosis

Dominant Genes

Recessive Genes

Instructions on next page

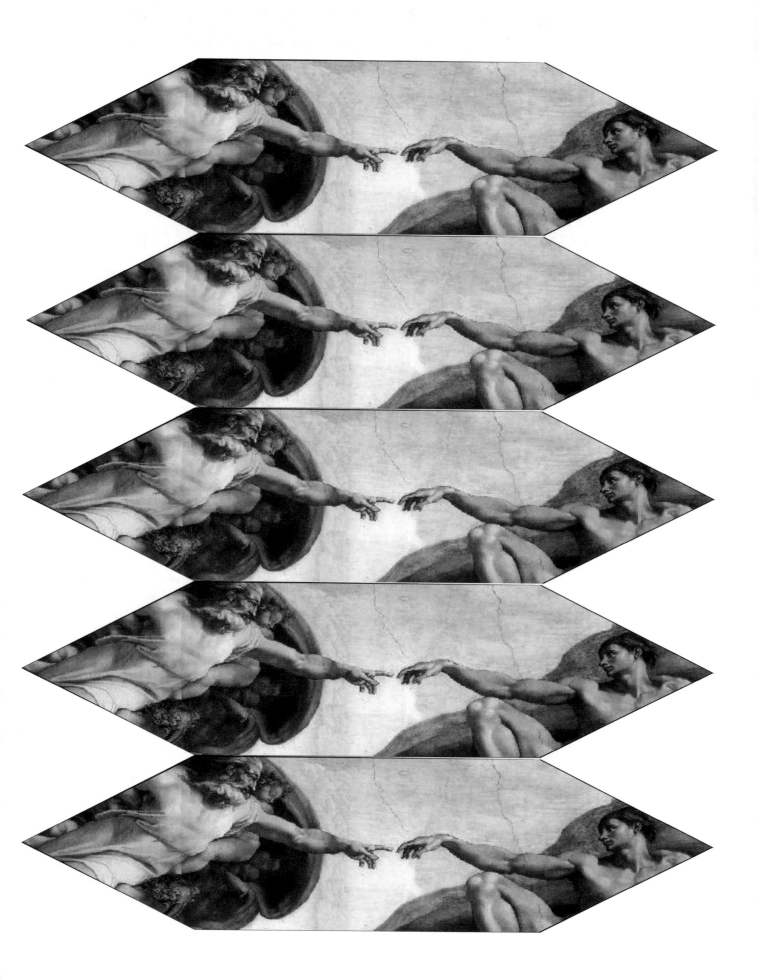

Growth and Development Fan: Lesson 14

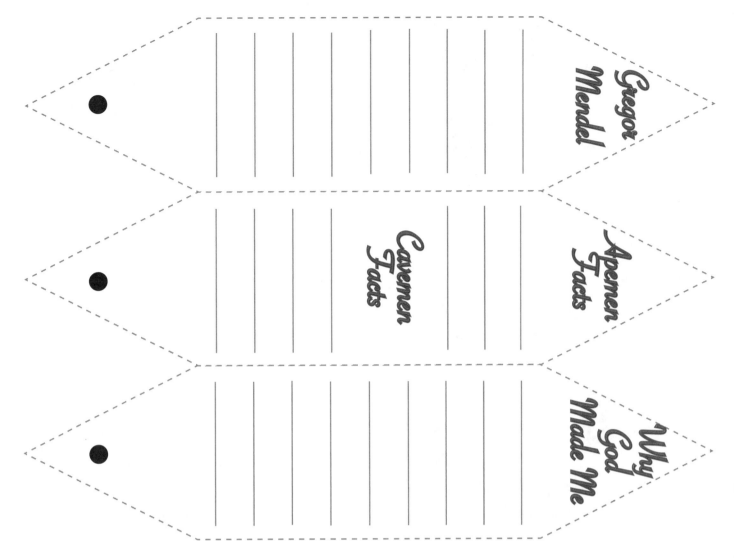

Gregor Mendel

Apemen Facts

Cavemen Facts

Why God Made Me

Instructions:

1. Cut out each individual fan sheet (on this page and the previous).
2. Punch a hole in the bottom of each fan sheet on the black dot.
3. Fill in the information requested under each topic.
4. Stack your fan sheets with the Creation of Adam image sheet on top.
5. Secure the fan sheets at the bottom by inserting a brass fastener into the punch hole.
6. Cut out the pocket to the left.
7. Put glue on the bottom and side edges and paste the pocket onto your "Growth and Development" paste page *(NJ p. 192)*.
8. Place your Fan in the pocket and remove it when you want to read all about Growth and Development.

Growth and Development Pocket

Growth and Development Fan: Lesson 14

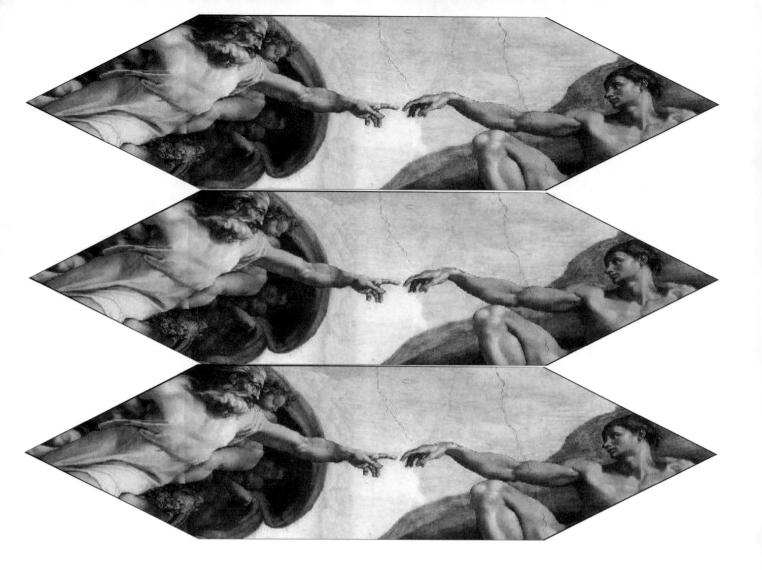

PERSONAL PERSON PROJECT

This section contains templates and illustrations for creating your Personal Person. Begin by choosing your body outline from the three colors offered here and on the next two pages. Next, add a photograph of your head to the top of the body. There are two body outlines for each color. The first outline will be placed on your Personal Person paste page (*NJ p. 15*). The second will be used in Lesson 12, after you study the integumentary system. As you work through each of the lessons, carefully cut out the organ or body system on the pages that follow.

Personal Person Body Outline (Lesson 1)

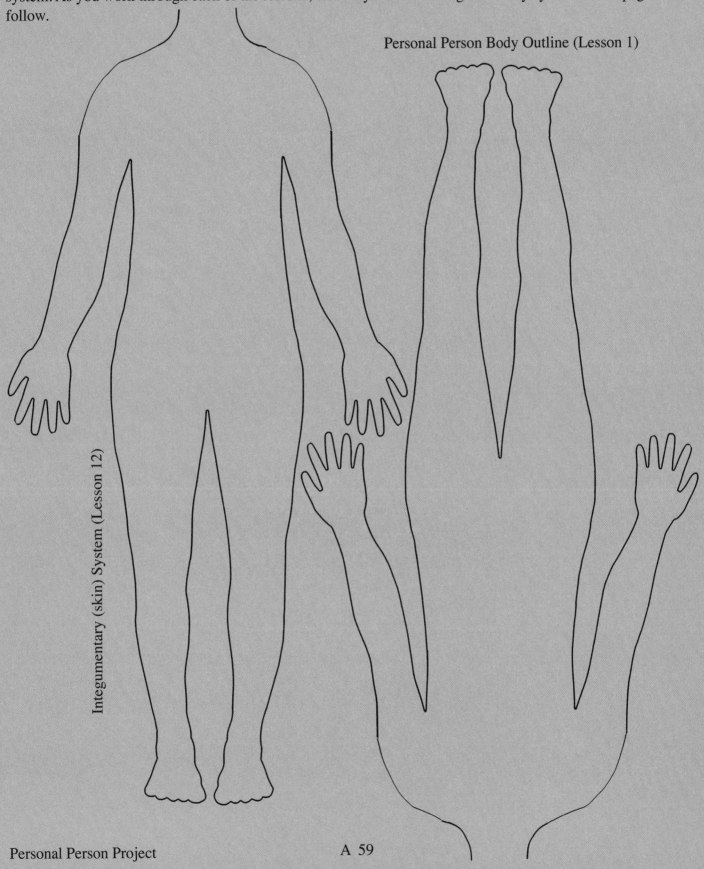

Integumentary (skin) System (Lesson 12)

Personal Person Project

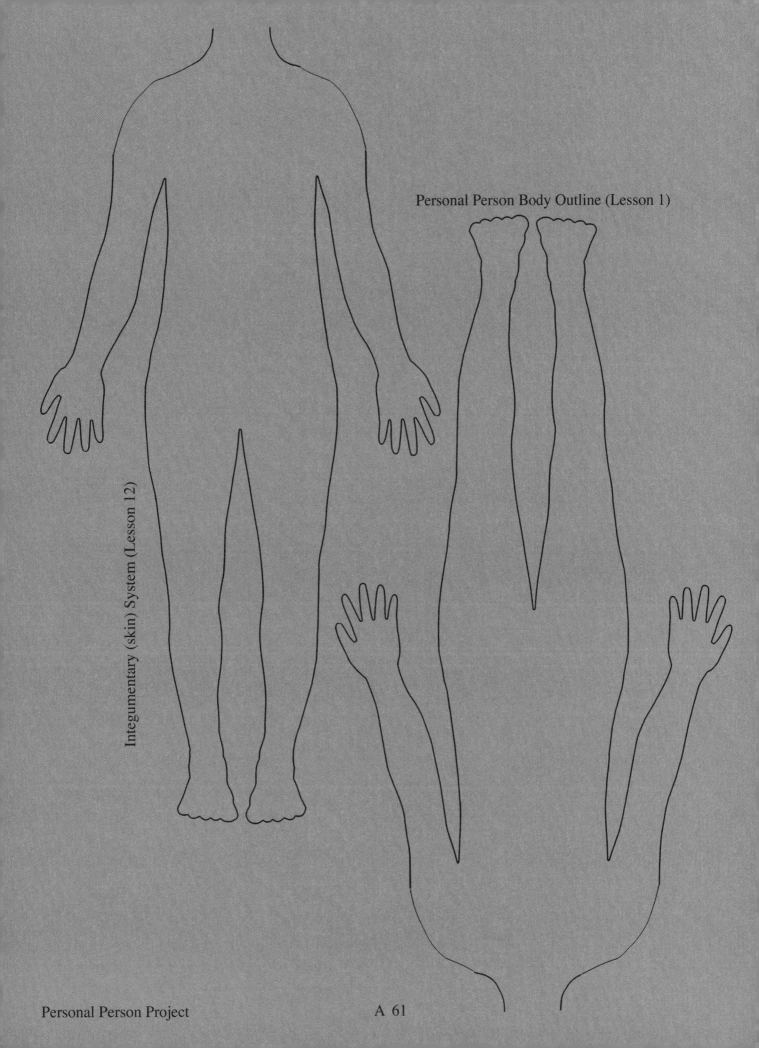

Personal Person Body Outline (Lesson 1)

Integumentary (skin) System (Lesson 12)

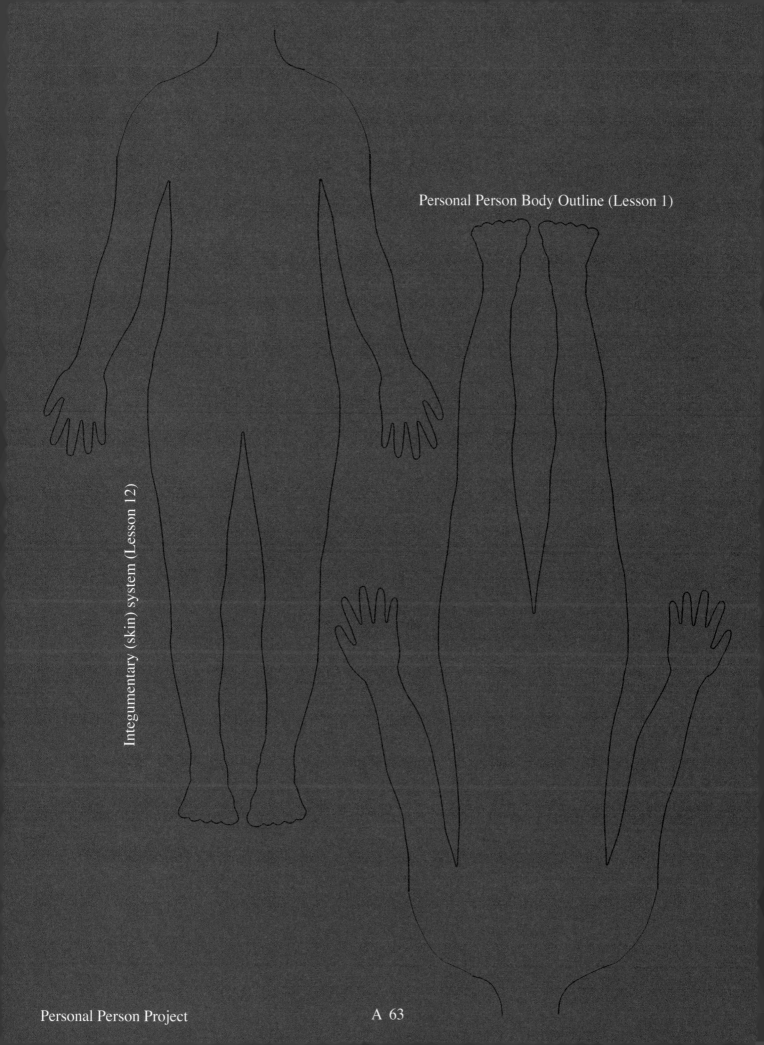

Personal Person Body Outline (Lesson 1)

Integumentary (skin) system (Lesson 12)